Financial Prosperity for People and Small Businesses Online: A Case Study

Dr. Ebenezer A. Robinson, PhD

ISBN # 13: 978-1496121486
ISBN-10: 1496121481

First Printing, 2014

Printed in the United States of America

Income Disclaimer

This book contains business strategies, marketing methods and other business advice that, regardless of my own results and experience, may not produce the same results (or any results) for you. I make absolutely no guarantee, expressed or implied, that by following the advice below you will make any money or improve current profits, as there are several factors and variables that come into play regarding any given business.

Primarily, results will depend on the nature of the product or business model, the conditions of the marketplace, the experience of the individual, and situations and elements that are beyond your control.

As with any business endeavor, you assume all risk related to investment and money based on your own discretion and at your own potential expense.

Liability Disclaimer

By reading this book, you assume all risks associated with using the advice given below, with a full understanding that you, solely, are responsible for anything that may occur as a result of putting this information into action in any way, and regardless of your interpretation of the advice.

You further agree that our company cannot be held responsible in any way for the success or failure of your business as a result of the information presented in this book. It is your responsibility to conduct your own due diligence regarding the safe and successful operation of your business if you intend to apply any of our information in any way to your business operations.

Terms of Use

You are given a non-transferable, "personal use" license to this book. You cannot distribute it or share it with other individuals.

Also, there are no resale rights or private label rights granted when purchasing this book. In other words, it's for your own personal use only.

Financial Prosperity for People and Small Businesses Online: A Case Study

6

Table of Contents

Chapter 1

Entrepreneurs of small brick-and-mortar businesses have shown a greater interest in using the Internet to expand small business profitability; but they lacked adequate procedures and risk assessments to mitigate barriers. This was because intense competition among sellers, places small and medium sized enterprises (SMEs) that had gone online in the last five years at a disadvantage. The problem explored in this holistic multiple-case study was that adequate procedures and risk assessments for barriers had not been implemented to eliminate the barrier of aggressive rivalry of sellers, which may impede the sustainable advantages for SMEs which had gone online since 2006.

This study was informed by the niche strategies of the Porter's theoretical framework. The purpose of this study was to ascertain whether procedures, risk assessments and business strategies could create sustainable advantages for people and SMEs that had gone online since 2006. A purposive sample of 20 online SMEs from multiple market segments was selected to inform the study.

Analysis of interview transcripts revealed three major themes: (a) the barriers to the operation of an online business, (b) the strategies used to mitigate those barriers, and (c) the methods that were utilized to maximize profit. The findings identified that entrepreneurs were experiencing complications in (a) procuring funding, (b) implementing risk assessments, (c) providing procedures, (d) obtaining repeat purchases, (e) retaining customers, (f) navigation glitch, (g) conversing with customers, (h) bonding with customers, (i) website traffic, (j) thin margin, (l) addressing computer illiteracy, (m) computer ownership, and others.

The results of the case study could help current or

new entrepreneurs to standardize procedures for overcoming barriers, maximize revenue, financial prosperity, and sustain competitive advantages. Recommendations resulting from this study included the following: aiming to improve profitability, joining an online barrier reducing associations, standardizing procedures, conducting periodic risk assessments, cataloging the internal controls for preventing barriers, indexing the methods for eliminating barriers, creating directory of online businesses, and distributing the directory to houses in United States. The completed research provided a theoretical contribution to the body of knowledge and scholarly literatures. In the United States, about 36% of adults have turned websites to procure clothing, accessories, shoes and services (Suki, Ramayah, & Suki, 2008). Fox (2008), Wong (2007), and Xu, Rohatgi, and Duan (2007) wrote that the online businesses expanded faster than all economic activities, especially manufacturing, merchant wholesaling, retailing, and selected service industries. Wong (2007) concluded that the transformation in each sector from traditional business to e-supported shipments, sales, and revenues was a gradual one (Wong, 2007).

Many online-business owners lack the proficiency and strategic vision to excel in online marketing and business engagements (*E-commerce Slows Again*, 2008; Fox, 2008; Wong, 2007; Xu et al., 2007). Aziz and Poorsartep (2009) and DotCom Boom (2005) stated that the owners of DotCom companies lacked business and marketing strategic skills. Aziz and Poorsartep found that online businesses overspent on information technology and marketing in the hope of maximizing profitability. For example, in 1999, Furniture.com generated revenue of only $10.9 million, but spent $33.9 million on sales and marketing.

According to Archer, Wang, and Kang (2008), major business trading partners have refused to conduct business with small- and medium-sized companies that are associated with online technology. Shook, Vlosky, and Kallioranta (2004) argued that the problem was related to financing and price management, which was the cause of the failure of many electronic marketplaces. Because of these problems, companies that started online failed; examples are bol.com, dot.com; paper industry.com; and datec.com (Constantinides, 2004; Lightfoot, 2003; Shook et al., 2004).

Despite these failures, online businesses are expected to expand by 500% through 2010 (Richards & Brown, 2006). New online business owners should be mentored by owners of successful online businesses (Eikebrokk & Olsen, 2009). In addition, new business owners should encourage consumers to purchase, and engage in up-selling and branding. Many studies have been done on electronic commerce, especially in customer relations, diversification, competition, advertisement, and growth (Campbell & Wright, 2008; Rau, 2007; Schmelz & Kennedy, 2004; Smith, 2005).

Online businesses are available to their potential customers 24 hours a day. The Internet has allowed small businesses that had once been limited by geography to their services or their products virtually anywhere. According to Wong (2007), regional products can now be sold nationally and in some cases internationally. At the same time, there are considerable barriers to making an online business profitable. Thus, this proposed research identified those barriers and how individual small business owners had surmounted them.

Background

The increased interest in using the Internet to expand small business profitability has not been the focus of much research. Specific studies have explored strategies for increasing profitability online (Choi, Kim, Kim, & Kim, 2006; Khalifa & Liu, 2007). In their study of online customer retention, Khalifa and Liu (2007) argued that online customer retention strategy is vital to profitability. A defined online customer retention strategy might help an organization gain repeat customers, thereby increasing their lifetime profitability to the company. An online customer retention strategy should include a multimedia design to enhance the virtual shopping encounter, free online trial versions and sample products. Managers or business owners should adopt the online shopping channel, use product enhancement and hire customer service representatives to convert customers.

Bansal, McDougall, Dikolli, and Sedatole (2004) argued that online companies need a user-friendly website that collects data and that makes selections and transactions easy. When consumers are satisfied with the online platform, the company will become profitable. Conversely, when consumers are not satisfied, online companies will not achieve profitability (Dikolli & Sedatole, 2007). Allen (2006) reported that 98% of online businesses have admitted that they do not know how to grow their profitability.

Gluhovsky (2009) suggested that strategic business models are necessary for procuring and increasing profitability of online companies. Gluhovsky (2009) reported that the online service provider should set the timeline to create and implement strategic business models. The service provider needs to increase subscription rates for clients who desire premium services (Gluhovsky, 2009).

Ashworth et al. (2006), and Childers and Offstein (2007) noted that online businesses face the problems of revenue deficits and insolvency. During the 1990s, global communities witnessed the following failures: (a) financial deficit of online businesses, (b) erosion of profit, (c) liquidations, (d) deficient decision-making process, (e) inefficiencies, (f) demise of online companies, and (g) aggressive competition associated with the digital environment (Childers & Offstein, 2007). Aziz and Poorsartep (2009), and DotCom Boom (2005) reported that 65% of online-business practitioners lack financial competency and 50% lacked online marketing skills. The side effects of incompetency had contributed tremendously to the liquidation of DotCom organizations.

Cattani, Perdikaki, and Marucheck (2007) suggested that the strategy of online competitors might influence both pricing decisions and profitability. For example, online grocers have adopted a variety of operations models, because profit in that industry is based on service and operations. Joia and Sanchez (2006) found that greater frequencies of purchases are not synonymous with increased profitability. Joia and Sanchez (2006) stated, "This issue is even more relevant when applied to e-commerce, in which industry-specific characteristics influence customer defection and profitability" (p. 5).

Online organizations need to establish accurate marketing communication and information in a form and time that improve its total performance (Yan, 2007). Online businesses can use marketing communication and information to respond more rapidly to customers' demand. Yan (2007) stated that accurate market information is vital to sustainable advantage.

Another factor in online business profitability is annual performance evaluations. Steinberg (2009) stated that online organizations should conduct annual performance evaluation on profitability and a final accounting of plan performance. McCue, Diana, and Hennum (2007) suggested that profitability is the result of a partnership between the employee and the employer. The process is often interactive and cooperative, thereby providing an avenue for a mutually beneficial and productive work environment.

As shown from the review above, a large amount of research had been conducted on the barriers to online business. However, none of the studies conducted focused on the barriers that could affect the profitability of small businesses that wish to conduct business online. This study examined the activities of small online companies and the importance of removing barriers to sustainable advantages. The qualitative data was collected using an in-depth interview questions with small business owners.

Problem Statement

The problem explored in this study was that adequate procedures and risk assessments for barriers had not been implemented to eliminate the barrier of aggressive rivalry of sellers, which may impede the sustainable advantages for SMEs which had gone online since 2006 (Aziz & Poorsartep, 2009; DotCom Boom, 2005; Gengatharen & Standing, 2005; Loghry & Veach, 2009; Porter, 2008). Online business owners face a much more difficult road to sustaining competitive advantages. First, customer loyalty may be more difficult when there is no face-to-face contact. Second, marketing strategies have to be different from those used for brick-and-mortar businesses because of the proliferation of online companies. Third, there is the ever-present threat of new entrants into the market, since unlike a brick-and-mortar environment; there is unlimited room on the web for new business entrants. In addition, it is less expensive to open an online business (Durand, 2006).

When SMEs decides to add an online component to his or her brick-and-mortar business, he or she encounters new barriers. While an online component of a business may initially generate profits, without careful analysis, that competitive advantages might disappear. There was a need to identify the barriers faced by SMEs when moving their business online. According to Antlová (2009), current business entities are forced to

14

consistently improve their products and services in order to attain competitive advantage. The managers of organizations have to utilize information and communication technologies and modern management techniques.

From the successfully growing companies which Antlová (2009) analyzed, he recognized the importance of business, information and knowledge strategy. Without verbalization of these strategies to the stakeholder and employees, managers or owners of SMEs will find it difficult to navigate their way through the current competitive business environment (Antlová, 2009). These strategies have to be followed by other supporting strategies, for example, marketing, finance and customer services (Antlová, 2009).

Purpose

The purpose of this qualitative holistic multiple-case study was to ascertain whether procedures, risk assessments and business strategies could create sustainable advantages for SMEs, (where the unit of analysis was the online SMEs market with multiple cases of individual online SMEs businesses) which had gone online since 2006. This study helped to understand the activities of small online organizations and the importance of eradicating barriers that may prevent sustainable advantages for small businesses. For the study, data were collected using an in-depth face-to-face interview questions with 20 small business owners. Varieties of market segments were chosen in order to mitigate the possibility of misrepresentation and elicit authentic evidence (Yin, 2009). The market segments that were integrated in this case study included technology, education, and home-healthcare, financial services, legal services, and automobile. This study therefore examined the barriers to online business profitability for small businesses as presented in the qualitative literature.

The findings of the study contributed to small business owners' knowledge of how to overcome barriers to online sustainable advantage. The experiences of 20 small business owners who decided to establish an online presence was gathered and reported. To attain rigor, Yin (2009) stated that an in-depth interview responses should be presented in a case study. The study key participants should be asked to narrate the facts and viewpoints of the phenomenon. The study participants should be encouraged to recommend other persons for interview and other sources of evidence. The more participants contribute value in this manner, the more they act as informants instead of as participants. Yin (2009) argued that key informants are often imperative to the success of a case study. Such informants provide the case study with both insight into and access to corroboratory or contrary source of evidence.

There was a need to explore the barriers faced by these SMEs when moving their business online in order to sell their products to customers in the United States. Thus, 20 small business owners who had taken their businesses online within the last five years were interviewed. The goal for this study was to suggest ways that small business owners could benefit from (1) websites selling, (2) online retailing, (3) online procurement, (4) online collaborating, and (5) online advertising. Similarly, these organizations may attain their advertising objectives by using Facebook, Twitter, Blogs, Podcast, YouTube, Flickr, Photobucket, and other online communities.

This study described prudent ways of building a profitable small online business. Profitability was defined as revenue minus expenses generated from the sale of products or services. This study explained the activities of small online businesses and the importance of eradicating barriers to profitability/sustainable advantages. The qualitative data was collected using in-

16

depth interviews through face-to-face, telephone, and e-mail with small business owners.

Theoretical Framework

The framework of this study is Porter's five forces of competition (Porter, 2008): supplier power, buyer power, competitive rivalry, threat of substitution, and threat of new entrants. Although all five of these forces exert pressure on a brick-and-mortar small business, the pressure to sustain a competitive advantage is even greater for an online business that does not have a single physical location.

According to Porter (2008), suppliers have the power to force business owners to pay higher prices. This ability to drive up prices is based on the uniqueness of their product or service. Businesses that have fewer choices of suppliers are more likely to have their competitive advantages. The factors associated with supplier threat are the number of suppliers, the quantity of supplies, the business' ability to substitute, and the cost of the substitution.

According to Porter (2008), a buyer may control the profitability of an online business. Porter maintained that buyer power is based on the number of buyers, their importance to the business, and switching costs. Businesses that have a few powerful buyers are more likely to control their prices. The factors associated with buyer threat are the number of customers, the size of the order, customer loyalty and lack of demand from customers.

Competitive rivalry may affect a business that has many competitors that offer comparable products and services. Although online business opportunities have a larger pool of possible buyers, they also have more competition for market share. For example, a small brick-and-mortar bakery that specializes in cookies might establish a web presence to increase its market share. According to Porter (2008), before going online, the business owner would have to identify other online bakeries and distinguish his or her bakery from them. The factors associated with competitive rivalry are the number of competitors, differences among competitors, customer loyalty and the cost of leaving the market.

Another barrier could be the threat of substitutes. For example, if that small bakery takes its brick-and-mortar business online in order to sell cookies, it might have to compete with companies that sell frozen cookie dough. A company that sells baking products might offer a free cookie recipe. The factors associated with threat of substitute include: (a) the performance of the substitute, (b) the cost of making the change to a substitute, and (c) the cost of switching to a substitute.

The final force in Porter's (2008) five forces model is the threat of new entrants. To return to the small brick-and-mortar bakery, the business owner will need to invest in a website, and hire either a website designer or have an employee do the work. Any competitor that is not online would need to do the same. A competitor that already has an online presence would not have these start-up costs. In the brick-and-mortar business, the threat of new entry would be limited in comparison to the threat of entry on the web. The web offers endless possibilities for market competition, so a business intent on moving online must gauge the extent of the threat of new entry. The threat of entry is tied to: the cost of entry, special knowledge required, cost advantages, economies of scale, technology protection, and barriers to entry (Porter, 2008).

To attain sustainable advantages for SMEs, Porter (1980) proposed competitive strategies: cost leadership, differentiation and niche strategies or (cost focus). The niche strategy is also a focus strategy. With a niche strategy, managers of SMEs concentrate on a narrow segment of a market. Competitive advantage is created exclusively for the niche. A niche competitive strategy is often used by smaller organizations (Porter, 1980). Managers of SMEs should incorporate lowest-cost business operations in that niche or segment. Porter reinforced cost focus as a viable strategy to achieve sustainable advantage. The managers of SMEs should integrate a competitive strategy of cost focus within the niche or segment. Porter (1980) argued that niche strategy increases sustainable advantages, market shares, higher sales, better margin and higher prices. The managers of SMEs may also adopt a differentiation focus, such as quality products, brand, customization to achieve sustainable advantages (Porter, 1980).

Porter (1980) demonstrated that cost leadership may help SMEs to achieve sustainable advantages. Cost leadership is driven by efficiency, size, scale, scope and experience. The managers who use lowest-cost operation to achieve sustainable advantages in the target segment should appeal to cost-conscious or price-sensitive customers. The management focuses on attaining economies of scales, customer satisfaction, customer services, product turnover, low cost supply chain and low cost delivery of products (Porter, 1980). The managers should train their employees on the principles of lowest-cost business operations. The managers are also responsible for cost containment. In order to attain sustainable advantages, the managers of these organizations should focus on the continuous improvement of their products and services in addition to innovations (Porter, 1980).

All of these forces affect a brick-and-mortar business owner's decision to expand online. Expanding the business by including an online segment can affect the competitive advantage of a small business that has a limited customer base. Although going online allows the small business to increase its customer base and market, it also presents many barriers to profitability. Small business owners need to apply Porter's five forces model when thinking about expanding their brick-and-mortar businesses.

Research Questions

The research questions determined the effectiveness of procedures and risk assessments implemented to eliminate the barrier of aggressive rivalry of sellers, which may impede the sustainable advantages for SMEs which had gone online since 2006. The barriers to online business sustainable advantages for SMEs across United States were explored. This study defines a small online business as one with approximately 100 full-time and permanent employees (Chitura, Mupemhi, Dube, & Bolongkikit, 2008). Campbell and Wright (2008) argued that aggressive advertising is the most important variable in the profitability of online business. It was important to determine if this claim holds true for small businesses. This qualitative study identified the barriers faced by small business owners when they move their service online. The following research questions were developed for this study:

Q1. What procedures, methods and risk assessments are used to eliminate barriers to online-business sustainable advantages for small business?

Q2. How are the procedures, methods and risk assessments implemented?

Q3. What are the procedures, methods and risk assessments monitored and verified?

Q4. What are the key problems connected with implementing the procedures, methods and risk assessments to eliminate barriers?

Q5. What primary internal controls (manuals or flow-charts) are used to eradicate barriers?

Q6. What profitability models and/or methods do online small businesses use to generate income?

Nature of the Study

In this dissertation, the problem explored was that adequate procedures and risk assessments had not been implemented to eliminate the barrier of aggressive rivalry of sellers, which may impede the sustainable advantages for SMEs which had gone online since 2006 (Aziz & Poorsartep, 2009; DotCom Boom, 2005; Gengatharen & Standing, 2005; Loghry & Veach, 2009; Porter, 2008). The purpose of this qualitative holistic multiple-case study was to ascertain whether adequate procedures, risk assessment and business strategies could create sustainable advantages for SMEs that had gone online since 2006. Twenty small business owners (adults over the age of 18) who had taken their businesses online within the last five years were interviewed. The 20 participants in this study were selected following purposeful sampling (Zikmund, 2003). The names of the SMEs who had moved to include an online component to their brick-and-mortar business were obtained from the United States Chamber of Commerce. All SMEs that meet the criteria were given the Informed Consent Form and Invitation Letter through mail or email to ask if they would like to participate in the study. The prospective participants were asked to read all documents, sign and return the Informed Consent Form. Those respondents that return a signed Informed Consent Forms were selected to participate in the current research.

The business owners who were interested in participating in the study were asked to return the Inform Consent Form via the self-addressed envelopes or email. The contact numbers of those who were interested in participating in the study was obtained. The participants were asked about the time they could be reached. To encourage responses from non-respondents, three email reminders were sent. Finally a personal telephone call was made. No further attempts were made to promote participation. A list was made up of those who returned the Inform Consent Form. If there were more than 20 participants, the responses were placed into a box and 20 folded papers were drawn. Those respondents were selected to participate in the current research study. Extra responses were kept in case some participants decided to withdraw.

After the participants were chosen, 45-minute interviews were scheduled. The participants were asked 34 open-ended interview questions. All interviews were tape-recorded with the permission of the participants. After each interview, the recordings were transcribed. At the completion of all interviews, the data collected were entered into a qualitative software program for data analysis. The qualitative software helped reduce the data to themes that can be reported. The participants informed this study with their subjective experiences, thought processes and converged on fact of the matter regarding the topic (Yin, 2009). The participants provided their viewpoints and interpretation pertaining to the barriers to sustainable advantages for online SMEs (Yin, 2009).

Leedy and Ormrod (2005) demonstrated that the academic communities must search for qualitative meaning units from the data they had collected. Similarly, after conducting data analysis, the results must accurately reflect the experience. For example, academic communities are known to analyze data collected from research studies, in order to emanate findings that counter criticism, bias, and distortion (Leedy & Ormrod, 2005). Patton (2002) reported that the qualitative data analysis and interpretations will allow for the conversion of data collected into themes, findings, theory, and recommendations. The study participants are channels for collected data; they generate communications, and explicate meanings about the study.

In order to ensure validity and reliability, this study enlisted a panel of three professors' comment on the interview questions. After IRB approval, a pilot test of the interview questions were conducted with two business owners to ensure that the questions elicit the type of information necessary to understand the barriers to online business profitability for SMEs. Trochim and Donnelly (2007) stated that academic communities should integrate the standards of credibility, transferability, dependability, and confirmability in order to integrate the authenticity of qualitative research. Yin (2009) concurred with Trochim and Donnelly's theory. Yin demonstrated that a pilot case study will help all individual to refine the data collection plans with respect to the content of the data, credibility, validity, and procedures to be followed. A pilot test was conducted on the self-designed instrument to develop relevant lines of questions (Yin, 2009).

Reliability of the findings was assured by having participants re-verify the interview responses in order to ensure that the transcripts accurately reflect what was verbalized in the current study. According to Trochim and Donnelly (2007), it is customary for academic communities to perform a thematic analysis of text, which identifies the themes or key ideas in a document or set of documents. The documents can take the form of field notes, newspaper articles, technical papers, and organizational memoranda (Trochim & Donnelly, 2007). For this dissertation, a qualitative software program, Nvivo 8, was used to group, code and analyze the transcripts so that the data from the open-ended interviews were developed into cogent findings, answer the research questions and append recommendations (Yin, 2009).

Significance of the Study

This research was to contribute and disseminate scientific knowledge about barriers to profitability of online small businesses. This was the first academic study of this topic. The research analyzed the problems and logistics in relation to profitability for online SMEs. A complementary objective of this research was to examine the barriers to sustainable advantage faced by SMEs that had taken their business online. This study presented best practices of building profitable online SMEs. Profitability of online businesses was defined as revenue minus expenses while engaging in transactions correlated with selling products or services. The purpose was to understand the experience from the participants' point of view. The appropriate qualitative design for this research was a qualitative holistic multiple-case study.

Definitions

To attain clarity in this study, the following terms were used:

Business-To-Business (B2B). B2B refers to business engagement between companies, rather than between a company and individual consumer (Laudon & Traver, 2006).

Business-To-Consumer (B2C). B2C is a type of business that uses Internet to sell its products or services to individual purchasers (Laudon & Traver, 2006).

Confirmability. The results discovered in a qualitative study can be verified by others than the creator (Trochim & Donnelly, 2007).

Consumer-To-Consumer (C2C). C2C involves consumers selling a product or service to other consumers. Popular websites like e-Bay, craiglist.org, thebarterclub.com, and xyzbarterexchange.com are good example of this type of Internet transaction (Laudon & Traver, 2006).

Field Research. The field research is a method by which academicians goes to a site in order to collect data for a topic under study. For example, marketing people often conduct field research by going to a public shopping mall, stopping potential consumers, and asking them a series of questions about a certain product or service (Trochim & Donnelly, 2007).

Mobile Commerce (M-Commerce). M-Commerce

refers to the application and services that are available when using an Internet-enabled mobile device. For example, mobile phones with Internet capabilities allow the user to find specific locations, e-mail colleagues, or purchase items (Laudon & Traver, 2006).

Online Business. These are businesses that have been created to sell products, services and to exchange information via the Internet. Some organizations are online only such as Amazon.com, while other businesses also have traditional retail outlets as well (*Encyclopedia Britannica*, 2009).

Peer-To-Peer (P2P). P2P allows Internet navigators to share with each other or transfer files to one another directly from their personal computers without using a website or directory (Laudon & Traver, 2006).

Profitability. This term refers to the amount of revenue that is earned from any business transaction after all expenses are paid. The equation for determining profitability is Profit = Total Revenue – Total Expenses (Investopedia, 2009).

Qualitative Data. Qualitative data, unlike quantitative data that describe data in terms of quantity, qualitative data are not numerical and are informal. Qualitative data usually involves information gathered from interviews or observations (Zikmund, 2003).

Unobtrusive Measures. The strategies employed personally to collect data without significantly interrupting the lives of participants who have volunteered to take part in the study. However, unobtrusive measures can limit the control the individual has over the data being collected (Zikmund, 2003).

Summary

There are many factors, such as customer-relationship management, marketing models, pricing strategies and quality management, involved in the conduction of an online business base (Xu et al., 2007). SMEs may face many barriers when they attempt to move their product or service on to a websites in order to expand their customer base (Xu et al., 2007). These barriers have not been the focus of research because SMEs trying to compete online with larger businesses are a rather new phenomenon (Fox, 2008).

Many owners of SMEs have not conducted risk assessments to secure a competitive advantage (Aziz & Poorsartep, 2009; DotCom Boom, 2005; Gengatharen & Standing, 2005; Loghry & Veach, 2009; Porter, 2008). Online managers are responsible for ensuring that the SMEs are integrating Internet business solutions to enhance their performance. The purpose of this study was to ascertain whether procedures, risk assessments and business strategies could create sustainable advantages for SMEs that had gone online since 2006. A central focus of the study was the strategies considered by entrepreneurs when determining the need to create sustainable advantages for SMEs that had gone online. This study was limited to barriers faced by online-business profitability for small businesses in United States. The manuscript provided insight that can be applied to other SMEs in United States. Therefore, the implication was that the finding of this study may not be applicable to other cities and states in the world.

Chapter 2

The purposes of this qualitative case study was to examine the barriers to profitability for SMEs, to identify gaps between prudent business practices, and the current marketing strategies in SMEs in United States, and to determine how these businesses could close these gaps. This study added value to the knowledge of the activities of online SMEs and the importance of removing the barriers to their profitability. The objectives of this study and literature review were to find resolutions to the research questions (problems). The literature was divided into the following subsections (a) Porter's five factor model, (b) online barriers; (c) capital barrier; (d) logistics and shipping barriers; (e) mitigating barriers; (f) barrier mitigating tools; (g) e-profitability models; (h) effectiveness of profitability models; (i) customer relationship management; (j) e-infomediaries; search engine optimization; (k) price and seal effects; (l) competition and prices; and (m) e-revenue and competition; (n) summary of the chapter, and they are contained in the body of this chapter.

In order to inform the research questions, the study cited the scholarly and peer-reviewed literatures. The literatures of the current study were obtained by using several keyword searches of the Northcentral University (NU) databases such as (a) ProQuest, (b) EBSCOhost database, (c) ABI/INFORMGlobal, and others. In order to conduct the study, the library of the NU website was accessed to download the literature, journals, articles, and magazines. The literature (or theory) collected from NU databases were rigorously perused and carefully compared to other existing studies to inform the current study.

Porters Five Forces Model

According to Porter's (1980a, 1980b, 1998), model can be used to identify whether new products, services, businesses, or industries have the potential to be profitable. Porter suggested that business owners look beyond their immediate competitors because other determinants of profitability need consideration. According to Porter, those determinants are the rivalry among sellers, the power exerted by customers, the impact of suppliers, the threat of new entrants into the market, and the threat of substitute products. According to Porter (1980b), the most significant of these forces is competition, which can be strong or weak. When a small business owner moves his or her business online, the number of competitors may increase dramatically, and products that are similar will compete based on price, endangering the new online business' profitability (Porter, 1980B).

Additionally, since there is no limit on the number of online business possibilities, there is always the threat of new entrants that can threaten the competitive advantage of established businesses (Porter, 1980a, 1980b). Brick-and-mortar business are often expensive to start-up so new entrants will be limited, but entry onto the web is relatively inexpensive for a new business. Hence, the threat of new entrants is a barrier faced by business owners who want to expand their brick-and-mortar business by adding an online component (Porter, 1980a, 1980b). According to Porter (1998), one of the most overlooked barriers is substitute products. Not only must a small business owner know what his or her competitors are selling, he or she must also be aware of what substitute products are available to customers. When the cost to consumer is low in switching to a new product the threat of substitute is high. Often companies may aggressively price their products when there is a new entry in the industry in an attempt to keep the customer from switching. When the threat of substitutes is high, the profit margin will tend to be low (Porter, 1980a, 1980b).

Two types of buyer power can also affect a business' competitive advantage. The first type of power is customers' sensitivity to price. If each brand of a product is the same, then customers will base their purchase decision on price. The other type of buyer power is negotiating power (Porter, 2008). Larger buyers have more leverage and thus can negotiate lower prices. When there are many small buyers, and all other factors are equal, the company supplying the product will have higher prices, and higher profit margins. The opposite is also true. If the company sells to a few larger buyers, those buyers will have the leverage to negotiate a lower price for themselves. However, if only a single supplier produces something a company has to have, the company will have little possibility of negotiating a better price (Porter, 2008).

Porter (1980a, 1980b, 1998) emphasized the importance of analyzing the five forces and their effect on a company. This analysis is especially important for small business owners who want to expand their brick-and-mortar business by adding an online element. Online businesses can face an intense competitive environment because Internet business can offer their products to a certain geographical area—like the United States—or offer their product to countries outside the United States. Online businesses are not limited by geography, but in the possibilities these online businesses offer, there is also barriers that must be faced and overcome if the new online element of the business is to sustain a competitive advantage.

Online Barriers

Karakaya and Stahl (2009) studied the barriers that confront online SMEs after they are integrated with e-commerce markets. Karakaya and Stahl presented information on imperative relationships between the barriers and firm performance. Small e-commerce organizations face scarcity of venture capital, Internet security, technical knowledge, and knowledge of conducting e-commerce, technology, infrastructure, and sustainability and e-commerce resources.

The sustainability barrier affects the competitive advantage. The e-commerce resources influence the profitability of online businesses. The barrier to e-commerce sustainability influences e-commerce resources (Karakaya & Stahl, 2009). The online SMEs may face sustainability barriers such as security of

29

financial transactions, computer hackers, not meeting customer service prerequisites, no access to distribution channels, and not meeting demand. The capital prerequisites barriers will influence sustainability. In addition, sustainability barriers manipulate the competitive gains of the rival online organizations (Karakaya & Stahl, 2009).

According to Karakaya and Stahl (2009), the entry barriers will permeate online SMEs even after e-commerce integration; the barriers usually affect brand loyalty, cost effectiveness, and low price. Karakaya and Stahl noted that barriers confront Internet banks after entering online market. In addition, online small firms and banking organizations will face barriers such as technical expertise, Internet security, competitors' actions, technical knowledge, and technology infrastructure (Karakaya & Stahl, 2009).

Karakaya and Stahl (2009) identified the dearth of literature on barriers faced by full-fledged small e-commerce organizations. Several entrepreneurs adopt e-commerce in order to accrue firm profitability. They discussed the competitive advantages of rival firms. They demonstrated that strong competitive advantages enjoyed by rival e-commerce firms (high barriers) generate e-commerce resources and lower firm performance (Karakaya & Stahl, 2009).

According to Karakaya and Stahl (2009), a strong competitive advantage emanating from strong resources can influence organizations with limited resources to feel mediocre. Despite the ease of entrance to e-commerce markets, sustainability barriers should be blamed for the lack of growth and profitability of e-commerce markets (Karakaya & Stahl, 2009). A capital prerequisite influences the competitive advantages and sustainability of the rival firms. Another barrier arises when a venture capitalist refuses to fund online SMEs. Conversely, the rival organizations with ample funding will enjoy greater competitive advantages. They conceded that capital requirements affect organization performance (Karakaya & Stahl, 2009).

Karakaya and Stahl (2009) demonstrated that SMFs should understand e-commerce resources barrier. These resources may include lack of technical expertise, inadequate e-commerce infrastructure barriers and a high learning curve (Karakaya & Stahl, 2009). Karakaya and Stahl (2009) noted that a stronger e-commerce resources or higher barrier is a precursor to a weaker organization financial performance. Karakaya and Stahl explained that e-commerce resources, the capital prerequisites, and the competitive advantages of rival organizations are more potent than sustainability barriers (Karakaya & Stahl, 2009).

The sustainability barrier has a covert negative impact on organization performance. In addition, Karakaya and Stahl maintained that sustainability barrier influences the perception of the competitive advantages of rival organizations (Karakaya & Stahl, 2009). When an organization's sustainability barriers are high, its management needs to see the competitive advantages of its competitors as high. Similarly, the sustainability barrier stimulates the perception of e-commerce resources, meaning that the higher the sustainability barrier, the higher the e-commerce resources barrier. The e-commerce resources barrier is a mediating factor here (Karakaya & Stahl, 2009).

Boyd (2003) argued that the Internet has eradicated natural barriers to competitive price information. By making price comparison available to customers, providers are making price comparisons among companies available to competitors. Virtual-time competitive price information is becoming a reality (Boyd, 2003). How should this data be used to enhance revenue management models? When this is not the correct revenue management model of customer behavior, as is happening, revenue, and optimization models need to be transformed. Boyd warned that using the wrong prediction and optimization models could reduce revenues (Boyd, 2003). MacGregor and Vrazalic (2006) found that females were more disturbed about e-commerce being inappropriate for their small business, while males conveyed more apprehension about the complexity of incorporating e-commerce into their small business.

Capital Barriers

According to Karakaya and Stahl (2009), profitable organizations admitted that capital requirements are the cause of barrier, followed by the competitive advantages of the rival organizations, e-commerce resources, and sustainability barriers (Karakaya & Stahl, 2009). The lack of e-commerce resources is attributable to lower firm performance, just as inadequate financing is a reason for failures of small business start-ups. Therefore, organizations should have excellent knowledge of e-commerce and adequate e-commerce infrastructure (Karakaya & Stahl, 2009).

The findings in this study specified that capital requirements or finances required could lead to sustainability, which influences e-commerce resources, and competitive advantages. Thus, organizations need to have the funds to maintain their e-commerce operations (Karakaya & Stahl, 2009). Although sustainability has no direct impact on organization performance, it has an indirect effect on financial performance through e-commerce resources. Thus, e-commerce resources act as a mediator. This denotes that a low sustainability barrier, combined with high levels of e-commerce resources, leads to higher firm profitability (Karakaya & Stahl, 2009).

According to Karakaya and Stahl (2009), capital requirements have no direct impact on organization performance, but it has an indirect effect through sustainability and e-commerce resources. Both sustainability and e-commerce resources are mediators in influencing firm performance (Karakaya & Stahl, 2009). Therefore, management must consider that capital requirements, sustainability, competitive advantages, and e-commerce resources are real problems that companies face in e-commerce markets. Overcoming these barriers with a strong plan for finances, infrastructure, human, and technical resources is likely to lead organizations to increase their markets in order to attain profitability (Karakaya & Stahl, 2009).

Logistics and Shipping Barriers

The electronic e-commerce executives found that organizations were accruing enormous additional revenues via their e-commerce efforts. An existing business let them subsist during the long period it was taking to grow the online segment of their business (Wresch & Fraser, 2006). Business executives faced substantial barriers to international operations, but every one of them was able to find option resources. Logistics, branding, security, and connectivity are all problems for these online business executives, but the innovative managers surmounted all the problems with minor difficulty (Wresch, & Fraser, 2006).

According to Room, Harrison, and Kerridge (2009), the relationship between non-effective accumulation and use of social capital which may inhibit access to proper decision-making circles, and limits the prospect of accessing critical management and financing resources, especially through the venture *capital* industry. Room et al. (2009) presented information on how SMEs who are growth oriented are hindered by lack of access to or control over such resources as, business premises, information and technology, production inputs, qualifications, experience, training facilities, and appropriate assistance from *business* development agencies.

Mitigating Barriers

Several profitable small organizations implemented a pricing plan and took a *strategic* viewpoint when setting prices. Strategies in the SMEs are often personalized and are induced by the actions, abilities, personality, and success criteria of the management (Beaver, 2007). A core finding in this literature was the value of strategic planning to small organizations. The managers in these organizations are governed by principle of continuous improvement. Without strategic planning, small organizations may attain profitability, but strategic planning simplifies comparisons with alternative futures, and opportunities (Beaver, 2007). Hodges and Kent (2007) found overwhelming proof that the managers of small organizations are persuaded that knowledge of strategic planning will bring profitability. Another finding of the study was that upper rates of sales growth were attained by small organizations that adopted sophisticated planning processes (Hodges & Kent, 2007).

Barriers Mitigating Tools

Chong and Pervan (2007) discussed that the fear of losing customers and market share may expedite organizational learning. The fear of expanding the use of new systems in order to keep up with competitors may also increase organizational learning. The appearance of competitive pressure will stimulate management to incorporate its business operations electronically both internally and externally with trading partners. Integration of these functions and trading processes is a matter of barrier elimination (Chong & Pervan, 2007).

Apigian, Ragu-Nathan, Ragu-Nathan, and Kunnathur (2005) stated that when organizations decided to use Internet technologies, they had reasons for doing so. For example, an organization may wish to increase its Internet sales in order to attain revenue expansion, by proffering an extra channel for marketing, and customer interaction (Apigian et al., 2005). They may not be initially enthusiastic about all aspects of Internet performance. Therefore, they focus on the elements that have the most direct significance for their business strategies (Apigian et al., 2005).

Online managers are using market channel available on the internet to enable revenue expansion. Several business executives are willing to interact with customers on the website in order to maximize profit (Apigian et al., 2005). Apigian et al. (2005) believed that revenue expansion (relationship enrichment and interactions) are analogous. According to Apigian et al. (2005), innovative managers are combining Internet-driven market channels, Internet interactions, and relationship enrichment to build relationship, and interact with suppliers.

Apigian et al. (2005) suggested that online organizations should integrate extra market channels and technology to ensure a personalized customer experience. This may bring about opportunity for expanded revenues and enhanced relationships between management, and customers. Apigian et al. (2005) advocated relationship enhancement by developing relationships with suppliers through Internet interactions. They indicated that by enabling real-time interaction with suppliers, customer could obtain instant feedback on any (customized, complementary products, or services) (Apigian et al., 2005).

According to Apigian et al. (2005), online managers are incorporating their internal system with one of these distribution carriers (such as FedEx) through a web-oriented interface, customer orders are instantly being assigned for pickup, and tracked in real time. To attain performance and cost effectiveness, the Internet instantaneously links customers to suppliers to guarantee swift delivery of products or services, and to allocate the receipt of the new order to internal employees (Apigian et al., 2005). For example, it may be more cost effective for online organizations to use companies like FedEx (or UPS) to deliver products to customers (Apigian et al., 2005). Customers can track their orders through these third-party distribution carriers, which also saves the company money (Apigian et al., 2005). First, by enabling Internet interaction with suppliers, the time and cost of searching for the right supplier or extracting data from current suppliers can be reduced. Second, the processing of orders, communications with employees, and administrative information can be greatly enhanced (Apigian et al., 2005). For example, e-commerce organizations can receive customers' orders, which are automatically processed by their system (Apigian et al., 2005).

Several organizations are integrating e-commerce to maximize sales and revenue. The management may assume that they are only offering an extra channel for marketing and customer interaction. E-commerce may not be profitable because the management may be reluctant to exert a total commitment and examine the performance of the e-commerce (Apigian et al., 2005). Antlová (2009) found that the organizations that use information and communication technology successfully have grown quite quickly. Several organizations are profitable because they have consistent operations; skill set, and knowledge strategies to derive competitive advantage. In addition, successful organizations use information and communication technology as a strategic advantage. In some organizations, the managers perform risk assessment, risk management, and audit to mitigate problems (Antlová, 2009).

E-Profitability Models

Coviello, Winklhofer, and Hamilton (2006) found that successful customer acquisition leads to profitability. Several organizations engage in database marketing, e-marketing and network marketing, but these efforts may

36

not attain or enhance financial performance. In the marketing practice-performance relationship, Coviello et al. (2006) found that communication marketing and transaction marketing affect performance.

Coviello et al. (2006) discovered that customer retention is positively correlated with interaction marketing; in contrast, customer acquisition is positively correlated with both interaction marketing, and transaction marketing. Managers are using interaction form of relational marketing to implement offensive and defensive strategies. On the other hand, managers may use transaction marketing to implement an offensive strategy. Customer acquisition is positively associated with sales growth; customer retention is not. Only sales growth (not customer retention) is positively correlated with profitability (Coviello et al., 2006).

Dembla, Palvia, and Krishnan (2007) suggested that the SMEs should assess their organizational structures and adopt web-enabled transaction processing technologies. Several managers are incorporating web-enabled transaction processing to maximize their customer base and minimizing transaction costs (Dembla et al., 2007). In order to do so, small organizations should invest in an information system to enhance their knowledge base, and acclimatize to new technologies. If the implementation of web-enabled technologies is prolonged, even organizations that usually operate in generic environments will have to integrate web-enabled technologies as they become pervasive. Dembla et al. also mentioned that the organizations that are fast growing and technologically sensitive will maximize revenue (Dembla et al., 2007). Garrity, O'Donnell, Kim, and Sanders (2007) argued that user-friendly computer tools should be configured by manager by embedding well-planned interfaces. The management should design web interfaces to bring satisfaction to customers, and simplify task process (Garrity et al., 2007).

Johnston et al. (2007) demonstrated that the SMEs are integrating Internet business solutions to enhance their performance. Internet business solutions incorporation accelerated and stimulated substantial financial recompense for SMEs in North America and Europe (Johnston et al., 2007). The recompense from Internet business solutions promoted revenue growth and cost effectiveness. Conversely, these financial rewards were not evenly disseminated across regions, industries, technologies, or size categories. The results suggest that SMEs managers should adopt a staged approach to Internet business solutions adoption in order to maximize profitability (Johnston et al., 2007).

According to Ashwin (2006), *guerrilla marketing* can be defined as the use of nonconformist marketing strategies to elicit the maximum exposure, attention, and results from negligible use of resources (Ashwin, 2006). Although *guerrilla marketing* has become popular, it is becoming difficult to negate the marketing strategies being used by small organizations with limited marketing budgets and the large organizations that have millions to spend on marketing (Ashwin, 2006). Managers often use guerrilla marketing by instructing small organizations to make contacts and build affiliations. Managers must be cognizant that every contact is a chance to promote the SMEs. This is 360-degree marketing (Ashwin, 2006). Managers can bring a product to the attention of prospective customers at the best time. Guerrilla marketing may elicit presence through chat rooms, email, forums, discussion boards, radio, magazine, street posters, and graffiti (Ashwin, 2006).

Small organizations are chronically short of cash to spend on marketing campaigns, so they can benefit from guerrilla marketing. The guerrilla marketing is small scale, flexible, and easy to modify. The marketing campaign can react to volatile or erratic marketing circumstances because guerrilla marketing is a cost effective and agile system of e-commerce marketing (Ashwin, 2006). With guerrilla marketing, the management must take care not to offend current and prospective customers. Some small organizations have negated this rule by intentionally provoking people whom they know are unlikely to be customers. Some organizations use controversy to attract the attention of their target audience (Ashwin, 2006).

The managers of e-commerce may use guerrilla marketing to target the communities that are most likely to purchase the product or service. The guerrilla marketing enhances the efficiency, return, and the e-commerce marketing campaign. Several managers have commented on how simple it is to use guerrilla marketing. The management will not spend a lot of money on guerrilla marketing (Ashwin, 2006). Guerrilla marketing has no bounds. There is no limit to what the managers can devise (Ashwin, 2006). The e-commerce organizations are known to use the Internet, pop up advertising, log-in details of visitors and advertise their brand on search engines such as Yahoo and Google (Ashwin, 2006).

Several managers of e-commerce organizations use blogs, banner advertising, sponsored links, stickers and badges, spray paint logos, and pavement chalking to promote their products and services (Ashwin, 2006). To advertise their online products or services, several managers of e-commerce organizations are legendary for using biodegradable posters, products give-away; free presentations; seminars; and intrigue-generating mystery (Ashwin, 2006). Peer marketing is another type of guerrilla marketing. The manager may even assemble people with similar interests or ages to build enthusiasm for the product. Roach baiting and buzz marketing are other forms of guerrilla marketing. The managers may hire actors to pretend to be customers to create interest in a product or service (Ashwin, 2006).

A popular form of guerrilla marketing is live commercials. Managers use people to conduct live commercials in clubs and pubs (Ashwin, 2006). With guerrilla marketing, several managers are enabling DJs (or club) events to advertise websites (Ashwin, 2006). Many small organizations benefit from the knowledge that will flow from boards of directors who have an academic background. The managers and the board of directors may even help the SMEs to access external knowledge from academic communities (Audretsch & Lehmann, 2006). The members of the board may help managers to solve problems so that the business has a competitive advantage in the market place (Audretsch & Lehmann, 2006). The resource theory of small organizations states that knowledge is a primary source of competitive advantage (Audretsch & Lehmann, 2006).

O'Dwyer and Ledwith (2009) found that business executives are innovating new products to enable organizational performance. Small organizations should be cognizant of their competitors, as competitor orientation is connected with both new product and organizational performance (O'Dwyer & Ledwith, 2009). The assessment of the performance of SMEs is problematic. There is hardly any objective data linking marketing action to business performance in SMEs (Simpson, Padmore, Taylor, & Frecknall-Hughes, 2006). Conversely, academics and managers have asserted that marketing activities enhance business performance (Simpson et al., 2006). The performance of SMEs is complex to assess because of normal flux in activities from year to year. This is exacerbated by the potential to influence the measures such as return on capital employed and return on investments that are used to measure performance (Simpson et al., 2006).

In SMEs, managers are responsible for assessing the operations that are profitable by subtracting total expenses from the total revenue of the organization.

Profitability is a matter of (a) operating profit, (b) net profit before interest and taxation, and (c) net profit before taxation (Simpson et al., 2006). According to Simpson et al. (2006), (a) net profit after taxation, (b) net profit after taxation, and (c) preference dividend, and all of these would render a different result (Simpson et al., 2006). In essence, managers should ensure that profit figures that will be used in ratio analysis are justifiable, consistent, and relevant (Simpson et al., 2006).

Several managers in SMEs are in favor of maximizing marketing operations when they determine the need for marketing. When the management anticipates that marketing efforts would be rewarded by increased revenue, they often will establish new market or the successful launch of a new product (Simpson et al., 2006). Although methodical overestimation was not found, managers did tend to create predictions that were too excessive, and likely to over extrapolate preceding growth. These outcomes are consistent with propositions that overconfidence biases and representative heuristics sway the revenue predictions created in small organizations (Cassar & Gibson, 2007).

Effectiveness of Profitability Models

Darbyshire (2008) performed a study on how to configure a framework for a web system that connects small and medium transport organizations with their customers (Darbyshire, 2008). With benefit and value for different organizations, Darbyshire noted that practitioners should consider the objectives of grouping several SMEs within the digital ecosystem (Darbyshire, 2008). A digital ecosystem is a self-organizing digital infrastructure aimed at developing a digital setting for networked organizations that maintains cooperation, knowledge sharing, and the creation of open and adaptive technologies, and profitability models (as cited in European Commission, 2004).

The management should amortize the cost of research and development over several groups of SMEs within the digital ecosystem. When the management amortizes the cost of technological development amongst players, it becomes viable (on a group basis) to execute further technologies which can add value to both SMEs and customers (Darbyshire, 2008). The cooperation among varieties of organizations should result in useful partnerships rewarding both SMEs and customers. SMEs are advised to form alliances and use each other's logistic chains and operation areas to offer more comprehensive services to online customers (Darbyshire, 2008). According to Darbyshire (2008), partnerships between e-commerce organizations are known as profitability models assisting the SMEs to compete more successfully in a growing global business. Darbyshire (2008) partnerships between e-commerce organizations are achievable because the architecture available in ecommerce ecosystem permits the SMEs to interface with larger external organizations (Darbyshire, 2008).

Several customers are recipients of recompense from added-value services in countless ways. The natural competition among cooperating SMEs in the digital ecosystem will drive transparent competitive pricing for the customers (Darbyshire, 2008). In addition, advantages to the customers from those of the SMEs will result in a vast range of services. SMEs can use each other's logistic chains and services (Darbyshire, 2008). Business executives are convinced that using logistic chains and services own by groups of SMEs in partnership will provide hub of access for customers, which is far more desirable than sourcing dissimilar services from several vendors. Managers stated that there is availability of vast market because of the capability of SMEs to connect with global carriers that have access to global market (Darbyshire, 2008).

Several organizations integrate value-added services such as parcel tracking and delivery notification to encourage customers to make repeat purchases. Conversely, such services would not be available through the selection of the initial bionetwork of the SMEs, but rather as result of further development. Nevertheless, such services would be added-value because of the architecture, and would not normally be reachable through SMEs operating alone (Darbyshire, 2008).

Distribution has undergone extraordinary transformations in the way that customers make their purchases. These transformations present new challenges as revenue management practitioners re-evaluate algorithms and create new models to account for web sales and competitive price information (cited in Boyd & Bilegan, 2003). Of course, not all revenue management challenges are connected to distribution. Contract revenues, groups, low-cost competition, tighter incorporation of forecasting, and optimization are just a few (cited in Boyd & Bilegan, 2003). Boyd (2003) said that distribution is the basis of some of the most pressing problems. Recognizing how fundamentally distribution affects customer demand and responds accordingly poses a key challenge for the future of revenue management (Boyd, 2003).

Boyd (2003) argued that organizations use the Internet because it is an extremely low-cost distribution channel. Boyd stated that using a computer operating system to drive sales on the Internet is far less expensive than using human intermediaries. The undesired repercussion of eliminating these intermediaries is that the current distribution environment is being altered (Boyd, 2003). For example, in the travel industry, customers would consult travel agents, who would purchase according to the sales agreements instituted with service providers. With e-commerce, customers can retrieve comprehensive information on dozens of hotels and rental cars in a matter of seconds (Boyd, 2003). Inventory control mechanisms have a natural propensity to become more complicated. The central reservation systems can quickly become a repository for intricate decision rules. The more intricate the control mechanism, the more likely there are to be unexpected communications among the rules, which may lead to an even more complex control mechanism (Boyd & Bilegan, 2003).

Revenue management and dynamic pricing issues are certainly related, and if the primary products are identical, the dilemmas are much the same. This relationship has created ambiguities in the way revenue management is operated, as is shown by the dichotomy in the way that forecasting, optimization, and control are treated by central reservation and revenue management systems (Boyd & Bilegan, 2003). Revenue management forecasting embraces a product archetype with a concentration on estimating demand by class. Conversely, with nested inventory control, whether for classes or virtual buckets is based on the premise of ordering products from high to low value with no overt regard for their defining characteristics (Boyd & Bilegan, 2003). The sale of inventory is quite different than for traditional revenue management applications, the conceptual predicament remains the same: estimate demand and its willingness to pay so that inventory may be managed to maximize profit. However, with so many inventories sold at discounts, the concentration shifts from short-term variable price to contractual terms (Boyd & Bilegan, 2003).

The success of revenue management in organizations has had a tremendous influence on the landscape for future e-commerce applications. The executives have found revenue management to be essential in generating profitability; it has paved the way for extensive adoption by industry (Boyd & Bilegan,

2003). The revenue management applications are being employed in the highly visible application of setting the price of airline tickets; it has helped popularize dynamic pricing. The managers of organizations are using the management application to execute dynamic pricing, revenue management, and to manage inventory against market demand to generate maximum profit (Boyd & Bilegan, 2003).

According to Boyd and Bilegan (2003), management must see beyond traditional applications to identify a rich collection of opportunities (Boyd & Bilegan, 2003). Contracts, alliances, collaboration, distribution, and the use of customer-level information present considerable challenges for revenue management, transactions, and the operations of organizations. The management should at least seize these challenges and make them work in operational e-commerce settings (Boyd & Bilegan, 2003).

Customer-Relationship Management

According to Yanamandram and White (2006), e-commerce organizations with low standards of customer satisfaction need to erect barriers to switching and comprehend the factors that encourage customer retention. Extra clarifications were given for customer dissatisfaction with failure of core service, price increases, and lack of flexibility in negotiations. Further explanations were given for customer discontent that included e-commerce organizations failure and poor customer service. The customers were also discontented because the e-commerce organizations failed to deliver on its promises of training customers who are computer illiterate and inability of service providers to help customers who are struggling with their finances (Yanamandram & White, 2006).

According to Yanamandram and White (2006), customers switched to other online companies because e-commerce organizations failed to solve their problems.

Yanamandram and White (2006) discovered that customer attrition occurs because there was a mismatch in organizational cultures. Several managers reported that customer attrition may materialize because customer representatives were indifferent or unresponsive to consumers. Several customers were frustrated because the online organization refusal to communicate with customers about delays. Additional reasons were given for customer dissatisfaction, such as e-commerce organizations' failure to understand customer expectations and not taking responsibility for problems caused by the service provider (Yanamandram & White, 2006).

Porter (2008) stated that profitable e-commerce organizations showed strong capabilities in Internet technology. The managers must implement a unique strategy for the e-commerce companies and other dot.coms. The management of e-commerce organizations must create customer value and charge for it, rather than depending on auxiliary forms of revenue (Porter, 2008). These organizations have distinctive ways of conducting physical functions and assembling non-Internet assets that correlate with their strategic positions. The e-commerce organizations support profound industry knowledge that permits the establishment of proprietary skills, information and relationships (Porter, 2008). Ratnasingam (2008) suggested that online managers should build (transaction, financial, business and interaction) relationships with their customers. The e-commerce organizations may need to waste time on customer who did not comply with procedures, and this created dissatisfaction with the organization and with the customer. Ratnasingam said that although shopping online may be a user-friendly process, organizations must periodically consult their customers to verify the effects of e-commerce customer-relationship management solutions on customer characteristics and behaviors.

Doherty and Lockett (2007) asserted that the correlation between relationship marketing (RM) and electronic customer-relationship manager (e-CRM) prevents technological challenges that will need to be resolved before organizations can reap the full potential of e-CRM projects. The rationale for this study was to impart new insights into ways of compensating for these impediments, and to closing the gap between the promise of RM and the reality of e-CRM (Doherty & Lockett, 2007). Doherty and Lockett (2007) argued that in order to be successful, e-commerce organizations should integrate a holistic perspective of relationship management. Doherty and Lockett noted that incorporating such a viewpoint means recognizing that while e-CRM technology may be indispensable for effectively meeting the challenges of RM, it is very unlikely to suffice on its own (Doherty & Lockett, 2007). The e-CRM technology eases the collection of high quality preference-related data from the customers, while automatically controlling marketing-oriented information to the customers. The managers are responsible for the success of the critical interface by satisfying and adding value to the customers. Doherty and Lockett (2007) demonstrated that managers must overcome RM technological challenges in order to enjoy the benefits of an e-CRM initiative (Doherty & Lockett, 2007).

E-Infomediaries and Search Engine Optimization

According to Palvia and D'Aubeterre (2007), an infomediary is a developing business model that organizations use in response to the vast increase in the amount of information available and the critical position of information in enabling e-commerce. Infomediaries perform a vital function by balancing customers' needs with organizations' products. There is a wealth of market data conveyed through the infomediaries as they carry out these functions. Consequently, infomediaries become a necessary path of knowledge about transactions in electronic marketplaces.

Palvia and D'Aubeterre (2007) studied the different infomediary functions in business to customer that pertain to automobile, retail, and travel organizations. Although the results identify the travel industry as one of the pioneers of electronic marketplaces, infomediaries in this industry do not demonstrate much incorporation and sophistication. In contrast, infomediaries in the retail industry demonstrate better integration and sophistication. This occurrence could be explained by disparities in competition in the travel and retail industries (Palvia & D'Aubeterre, 2007).

According to Palvia and D'Aubeterre (2007), the travel industry is administering organizations such as Sabre, Travelocity, Microsoft Expedia, and Orbitz.com. The retail industry does not have such sophisticated organizations. The lack of severe competition in the travel market allows infomediaries to be reactive instead of proactive. Conversely, infomediaries on the retail market should combat the competitors (Palvia & D'Aubeterre, 2007).

Offstein and Childers (2008) found that the theoretical viewpoint best suitable to explaining entrepreneur deed was based on the business owner's attributes, traits, and dispositions. Offstein and Childers argued that comprehending the drivers of e-commerce adoption, policy makers and other helping agencies can modify programs to assist small organizations with integrating and exploiting e-commerce cost-effectively. Offstein and Childers indicated that the success and continued involvement of the nation's small businesses are essential to the long-term viability of the U.S. economy.

Online managers should have excellent knowledge of search engine optimization and should fully utilize their web site as a tactical strategic marketing tool

(Murphy, Catherine & Christian, 2008). According to Dawson and Hamilton (2006), who posited that online managers have the capability to amend the parameters of search engine optimization, if necessary, reconstruct the entire keywords for visibility, ready for the next customer visit from Google robots. The managers of the online grocery stores have incorporated search engine optimization strategies to enhance the brand image of the company. Small businesses would derive brand exposure by incorporating search engine to maximize consumer conversion rate, increase revenue per visit, and secure competitive advantage (Gofman et al., 2009).

Vachon (2011) suggested that online managers should utilize search engine including several non-cognitive decision-making tools to attract consumers to visit their web site. Vachon asserted that the search engine optimization should be configured to be user-friendly and guide the target audience to precise navigation venue. Vachon articulated that search engine should be adapted to the varieties of products offered in each web store. Online managers are enabling search engines to assist customers to implement their decision on the websites (Vachon, 2011). Quinton and Mohammed (2009) found overwhelming proof that the manager use search engine optimization, press release distribution and directory submission tools to stimulate customer traffic to their web site. Quinton and Mohammed concentrated on understanding the role of SMEs organizations and their use of search engine optimization to attract web site traffic (Quinton & Mohammed, 2009).

Price and Seal Effects

As web seals are known to assist and motivate some customers to buy from less-established e-commerce vendors, a lower settlement price is offered to these shoppers, and social welfare (well-being) might be enhanced as a result (Hu & Wu, 2008). Hu and Wu concluded that the price effect, the seal effect, and the reputation effect are accountable in decision-making process of online customers. When the online environment is presumed to be risky, reputation effect plays a major role, and customers frequently purchase from well-established e-vendors only (Hu & Wu, 2008).

As the assumed proportion of trustworthy e-commerce vendors among less-established ones increases the seal effect starts to play a major role (Hu & Wu, 2008). Hu and Wu (2008) found that online managers are enabling web seals on the website to portray their organizations as authentic businesses. Hu and Wu (2008) found that small e-commerce vendors with seals start to lure customers from the well-established e-commerce vendors. In fact, when the price advantage is high and when online trading is presumed to be less risky, customers prefer to purchase from a less-established e-commerce vendor without seal than from a well-established e-vendor (Hu & Wu, 2008).

Hu and Wu (2008) found that the price effect is the main factor that draws customers to small e-commerce vendors. The involvement of small e-commerce vendors and the web seals is responsible for the intensive competition in e-commerce markets and contributes to social well-being (Hu & Wu, 2008). Consequently, customers now benefit from lower prices, low reputation e-vendors have privileges to compete in e-markets, and social well-being is enhanced as e-markets become more competitive and secure (Hu & Wu, 2008).

Usability on the Internet should simplify the design of web pages and make them user-friendly. According to the International Organization for Standardization, the term *usability* means that the capability of software products is not widely understood, learned, used, and attractive. Another definition of *usability* is the extents to which prospective and current customers are embolden to easily access a product on the websites (Guerrero, Egea, & González, 2007).

Usability has become a prerequisite for effective e-commerce websites, especially as the Internet spreads to consumers with less computer experience. Shopping websites must be customer-oriented if customers are to navigate the sites (Guerrero et al., 2007). In this regard, usability is invaluable to increase website reliability and user satisfaction. The problems of usability often deter prospective and current customers from participating in shopping spree (Guerrero et al., 2007).

Competition and Prices

In comparison shopping markets, products are the same and the barriers to access and exit are insignificant. Therefore, market concentration and information will determine market structure (Saastamoinen, 2009). According to Saastamoinen (2009) market structure determines pricing and profits, studying data from comparison in e-commerce shopping markets assist managers to understand how market concentration and information arrange competition in e-markets (Saastamoinen, 2009).

The evidence reveals that the number of sellers in the market has a great impact on pricing. More precisely, the number of storefronts seems to affect more than the number of sellers (Saastamoinen, 2009). As storefronts sell their products through the comparison-shopping website, they are more likely to enter into price competition. For other sellers, a comparison-shopping website attracts more price-conscious customers because they may derive a large bulk of sales elsewhere. For this reason, these online sellers have no interest in entering price competition in order to avoid bargain-hunting consumers (Saastamoinen, 2009).

The findings of this study provide information about the importance of a seller's reputation in highly competitive online comparison shopping markets. For SMEs, a commitment to staying in the market, as reflected in the organization's ratings history, may provide some pricing power. Large, e-commerce organizations seem to benefit from their reputations (Saastamoinen, 2009). In light of this evidence, organizations should not overvalue the competitive advantage of a good reputation. It is likely that as long as a seller does not diverge significantly from its peers, customers overlook small differences in reputations and prefer lower prices (Saastamoinen, 2009).

The managers are cognizant that active reputation maximization is not effective in enhancing a competitive advantage in shopping markets because the main objective is to enable consumers' price search across vendors (Saastamoinen, 2009). In contrast, the low price strategy may help SMEs to earn consumer trust. As SMEs become established online sellers, they can set small price premiums over market entrants (Saastamoinen, 2009).

E-Revenue and Competition

There is little evidence to support the premise that a firm's revenue correlates to the effectiveness of its e-commerce supply chain management efforts. As technology has advanced, e-commerce supply chain has become important to organizations. In the global economy, today's business setting is more competitive than it was in the past (Lancaster, Yen, & Yuan Ku, 2006).

Relationships throughout the supply chain are essential to a thriving organization. Improved communications among trading partners can elicit quicker analysis, feedback and solutions to inventory and customer service anomalies. Yet, organizations trying to administer their supply chains still encounter problems. Perhaps the most critical issues in supply chain management are mistrust and competition (Lancaster et al., 2006). Simultaneously, knowledgeable customers are another barrier to organizations that are not competitive. Customers who are displeased with one company can easily find a more satisfactory one. Organizations are now confronted with more customers that are difficult to satisfy and retain (Lancaster et al., 2006).

The dot-coms e-commerce organizations were renowned for their personalized online shopping experiences. Their websites reflect their customer focus. They offer a vast amount of information and data on their customers, which can be used to create custom storefronts when customers return (Lancaster et al., 2006). These companies also promise excellent response time, and in several cases, this responsiveness is a manifestation of their efficient supply chain. All of the websites offered some form of personalization, accessed by creating an account and accessing it via the use of a login and password. Amazon.com permits its suppliers to create virtual shelves, with a shopping cart, and a vast inventory (Lancaster et al., 2006).

Summary

Karakaya and Stahl (2009) presented information on barriers that confront online small organizations after they have been integrated with e-commerce markets. They explicated the relationships between barriers and firm performance. Small e-commerce organization faces scarcity of venture capital, Internet security, technical knowledge, knowledge of conducting e-commerce, technology, infrastructure, sustainability, and other resources (Karakaya & Stahl, 2009; Arcand, Nantel, Dufour & Vincent, 2007).

The component of several online organizations included small markets and small numbers of competitors in most sectors, resulting in low levels of competitive rivalry, threat of new entrants, threat of substitute products (services), and bargaining power of buyers resources (Loukis, Sapounas, & Aivalis, 2008). However, in some sectors there are small numbers of prospective suppliers, so these suppliers are in a strong bargaining position, which results in high prices for basic inputs, creating intense pressures to develop valuable efficiency-oriented applications, and a more efficient use of information communication technology (ICT) resources (Loukis et al., 2008). Loukis et al. (2008) demonstrated that among the five forces of Porter's framework, only the bargaining power of supplier affects ICT business value. Loukis et al. (2008) concluded that the higher levels of bargaining power of suppliers generate big pressures for the development of efficient applications, and a more efficient use of ICT resources, increasing the contribution of ICT investment to output (Loukis et al., 2008).

Malaga (2007) demonstrated that search engine optimization is an effective strategy for improving search engine brand equity, web site traffic and consumer conversion. Malaga (2007) found that the search engine optimization project provided evidence of cost effectiveness than the pay-per-click campaign. Visser and Weiderman (2011) found that the implementation of search engine optimization is imperative to improve brand rankings and that website usability attributes are imperative to increase customer conversions and return on investment. In agreement, Malaga (2007) asserted that search engine optimization often provide return on investment for online SMEs. Visser and Weiderman (2011) stated that the inclusion of the website usability attributes positively influence customer retention. Visser and Weiderman (2011) concluded that online usability is a requirement for effective website design.

Those SMEs that have survived market/economic barriers, prospered and expansion demonstrated most or all of the subsequent attributes. First, the managers of the small organizations had a rigid grip on their finances and cash flows (Beaver, 2007). Second, the management scrutinized business projections vigilantly, elicited sound decisions, and adapted strategic management. Third, the management of small organizations revisited their original business plan in order to enhance primary conjectures made about sales volume and cash flow (Beaver, 2007).

Room et al. (2009) presented information on how small business owners who are growth oriented are hindered by lack of access to or control over such resources as, business premises, information and technology, production inputs, qualifications, experience, training facilities, and appropriate assistance from *business* development agencies. Room et al. (2009) discussed the relationship between non-effective accumulation and use of social capital which may inhibit access to proper decision-making and limits the prospect of accessing critical management, and financing resources, especially through the venture *capital* industry.

Harris and Rae (2009) found that the e-commerce technology has reached the point where the entry costs and barriers to remote and collaborative working have disappeared into thin air. Gifted online managers can acquire marketing skills and learn about secure information technology systems, in addition to the capability to network and collaborate globally on projects, by generating virtual (and even disposable) organizations without having to rely on a traditional information technology infrastructure. Harris and Rae concluded that business owners can avoid dependence on information technology suppliers and grow their *businesses* in more flexible ways.

Harris and Rae (2009) found that online managers who are talented and proactive can promote the brand through blogging, networking and judicious use of search engine optimization techniques. Online managers are now competing against larger organizations. Online managers should apply network effects to their marketing activities and operations. According to Harris and Rae (2009), several managers are circumventing the need for complex information technology systems by using cost-effective Web 2.0 tools and enhancing their own networking proficiency. Hettche and Walker (2010) presented an overview on collaborative competition between small business and small nonprofits organization serving as a model for thriving collaboration. Hettche and Walker (2010) argued that SMEs can remain competitive in both converging and pluralistic market environments. Hettche and Walker concentrated on understanding the importance and role of intellectual capital for community service, and creative free trade.

Rauyruen, Miller and Groth (2009) examined how customer retention is a main way of achieving high profitability and maximizing revenue. When competent managers retain customers, firm performance may be enhanced by repeat purchases, charging more for products and services, and enhancing brand equity. Hu and Wu (2008) focused on marketing and economic value that can be implemented by adding a web seal to the e-commerce site. Because of the nature of electronic commerce, it is difficult for consumers to determine the trustworthiness of an online merchant, especially when an online organization is small and less established. Hu and Wu discussed the conditions under which some organizations used a third-party-assured web seal to build trust. Although seals of approval have a long offline history, the use of web seals is a recent phenomenon.

The management establish a decision making model to be undertaken to achieve the objectives and how the processes are to be accomplished. The online managers and customer services representatives are responsible for scrutinizing and communicating with the online customers when they would choose to procure from a small less-established online retailer rather than from a well- established one. This model shows that when the same product can be acquired from either a less-established online retailer or a well-established online retailer, comparative price advantage draws customers to the less-established online retailers. Small online retailers compete with big retailers on the basis of price (Hu & Wu, 2008).

Hu and Wu (2008) found that the reputation effect (price effect, the seal effect) affect an online customer's decision making. When the online environment is perceived as risky, reputation effect plays a major function, and customers rely on well-established online retailers. As the perceived proportion of honest online retailers among less-established ones increases and the use of Web seals change a great number of strategic online retailers into more accountable businesses, the seal effect starts to play a major function. Small online retailers with seals lure customers from more established online retailers. In fact, when the comparative price advantage is high and when online commerce is perceived to be less risky, customers would rather purchase from a less- known online retailers with no seal (Hu & Wu, 2008).

According to Hu and Wu (2008), the price effect attracts customers to online SMEs. From a social planner's viewpoint, participation of small online retailers and the use of Web seals encourage competition in e-commerce, which enhances social welfare. As a result, Hu and Wu (2008) found that consumers benefit from lower prices, unknown online retailers can compete with competitors and social welfare is enhanced as e-commerce becomes more competitive (Hu & Wu, 2008).

Chapter 3

The problem explored in this qualitative holistic multiple-case study was that adequate procedures and risk assessments for barrier elimination had not been implemented by many managers and owners of SMEs.

These procedures were necessary to eliminate the barrier of aggressive rivalry of sellers, which may impede the sustainable advantages for SMEs which had gone online since 2006 (Aziz & Poorsartep, 2009; DotCom Boom, 2005; Gengatharen & Standing, 2005; Loghry & Veach, 2009; Porter, 2008). Online managers are responsible for ensuring that the SMEs are integrating Internet business solutions for SMEs in United States to enhance their performance and sustainable advantages. Internet business solutions have accelerated and stimulated substantial financial recompense for SMEs in Europe (Johnston et al., 2007).

Johnston et al. (2007) demonstrated that business executives are responsible for providing managerial oversight and conduct management reviews of the procedures and for ensuring that Internet business solutions promote revenue growth and cost effectiveness (Johnston et al., 2007). Conversely, these financial rewards were not evenly disseminated across regions, industries, technologies, or size categories. The results suggest that SMEs managers should adopt a staged approach to the adoption of Internet business solutions in order to maximize profitability and attain sustainable advantages (Johnston et al., 2007).

Chong and Pervan (2007) asserted that SMEs assume that early integration of their operating system between the organization and its trading partners may preclude the likelihood of the trading partners discovering a more attractive competitive relationship. By being more proficient in business transactions with their partners through faster and more accurate processing, the competitiveness of SMEs would be strengthened. In brief, better correlations with the prospective and current customers of SMEs would be formed (Chong & Pervan, 2007).

According to Dembla et al. (2007), online managers should assess their organizational structures in order to integrate web-enabled transaction processing technologies. SMEs would derive sustainable advantage by incorporating these technologies to maximize their customer base and minimize transaction costs (Dembla et al., 2007). In order to do so, SMEs should invest in an information system. If the trends of implementation of web-enabled technologies continue, even organizations that operate in generic environments should integrate web-enabled technologies as they become pervasive. According to Dembla et al. (2007), organizations that are fast growing and technologically sensitive will make the greatest advances.

The purpose of this qualitative holistic multiple-case study was to ascertain whether procedures, risk assessments and business strategies could create sustainable advantages for SMEs that had gone online since 2006. This study helped to understand the activities of online SMEs and the importance of eradicating barriers that may prevent sustainable advantages for SMEs. Multiple qualitative data and evidences were collected using interviews with 20 SMEs owners (Yin, 2009).

According to Loghry and Veach (2009), the managers have the inherent duty to conduct an annual or quarterly risk assessment of business operations. Each organization is ever-changing and changes that influence any exposure, susceptibility, barriers, and threat must be addressed in a risk assessment review. Risk assessment is not a panacea, whether created by private industry or the government. Loghry and Veach (2009) argued that performing risk assessment of the potential for losses to an organization can be regarded as an excellent risk management than no risk assessment at all (Loghry & Veach, 2009). Several managers are using internal control standard to manage and eliminate risk. The managers are responsible for introducing internal

59

controls to minimize risk (Khattab, Aldehayyat, & Stein, 2010).

The purpose of this qualitative holistic multiple-case study design was to explore barriers to sustainable advantages for SMEs that had gone online in United States. This study could help academic communities to understand the activities of online SMEs and the importance of eradicating barriers that may prevent online business profitability for SMEs. The qualitative data was collected using in-depth interview medium such as face-to-face, telephone, and email with 20 online SMEs owners in United States.

Smolander and Rossi (2008) argued that the key impediment to the growth of e-business is in maintaining day-to-day operations and in incorporating legacy systems into the new e-business functionality. Shook et al. (2004) emphasized that several online organizations including the Global Forest Company faced liquidation because the managers did not integrate two-way communication with the customers. In this dissertation, the kind of problem best suited for qualitative holistic multiple-case study design was the one that describes a real-life phenomenon. A case study examines a contemporary phenomenon from the premise of depth and context, especially when the limits between phenomenon and context are not evident (Yin, 2009).

This study adopted a qualitative methodology in order to examine the barriers faced by SMEs owners when they take their business online. Twenty SMEs owners were interviewed to identify some of these barriers. The findings of this qualitative study exhibited the experiences and business worldview of online SMEs. The current study was designed to clarify, and convert the findings into new knowledge, and recommendations. This dissertation made a theoretical contribution to the body of knowledge.

The research questions determined whether adequate procedures and risk assessment had been implemented. The following questions were used:

Q1. What procedures, methods and risk assessments are used to eliminate barriers to online-business sustainable advantages for small business?

Q2 How are the procedures, methods and risk assessments implemented?

Q3 How are procedures, methods and risk assessments monitored and verified?

Q4 What are the key problems connected with implementing the procedures, methods and risk assessments to eliminate barriers?

Q5 What primary internal controls (manuals or flow-charts) are used to eradicate barriers?

Q6 What profitability models and/or methods do online small businesses use to generate income?

The results of this study assisted small online businesses in improving their online business prospects. The 20 participants in this study were selected following purposeful sampling. The participants were knowledgeable business owners who are citizens of United States. According to Zikmund (2003), purposive sampling is a non-probability sampling method in which an individual selects the sample based on his or her judgment about appropriate characteristics needed of the sample members. Yin (2009) emphasized that other academicians should be able to replicate the findings and conclusions of the case study. Yin (2009) stated that collection of multiple evidence and replications of conclusions are imperative in the case studies as opposed to sampling methods.

This study answered the research question by using data collected from interviews with 20 SMEs owners who had expanded their businesses online. The participants were interviewed for approximately 45 minutes. All interviews were tape-recorded and transcribed into Nvivo 8, qualitative software, so that themes can be developed for reporting of the data. The purpose of this qualitative study was to interrogate the participants and collect (interview responses, experiences, meanings and notes) to find answers to the research questions (Yin, 2003; Yin, 2009). The purpose of this qualitative holistic multiple-case study was to interview the participants and collect (opinion, texts, chain of evidence and audio data) to find resolutions to the research problem and questions (Yin, 2003; Yin, 2009).

Research Methods and Design(s)

The design that was selected for this dissertation was a qualitative holistic multiple-case study. The unit of analysis was the online SMEs businesses with multiple cases of individual SMEs in United States. The unit of analysis (20 participants) was selected following purposeful sampling (Zikmund, 2003). The names of the prospective participants were obtained from the United States Chamber of Commerce. To address the research questions, the interviewer captured the personal experiences of the unit of analysis to resolve the research problems. In this study, the qualitative holistic multiple-case design was organized to achieve the research purpose and elicit overall explanation. This design focused on replication approach of multiple case studies. Yin stated that any implementation of qualitative holistic multiple-case studies should follow the concept of replication without adhering to sampling logic. Yin asserted that academic communities are known to peruse and select each case carefully to elicit validity and reliability (Yin, 2003; Yin, 2009).

The qualitative holistic multiple-case design was used to analyze multiple data (evidence) to integrate (imperative statements, pattern matching, explanation building, logic) pertinent to barriers to online business profitability for SMEs (Yin, 2003; Yin, 2009). Yin (2009) posited that academic communities should formulate a theoretical framework whenever they are intending to conduct a case study. A good case study should formulate the theoretical framework, no matter whether the study is to be explanatory, descriptive or exploratory. In conducting cases studies, Yin (2009) found that the integration of theory is an immense aid in defining the appropriate research design and data collection. The same theoretical direction also becomes the most imperative vehicle for generalizing to new cases (Yin, 2009).

The framework of this study was guided by the Porter's five forces of competition (Porter, 2008): competitive rivalry, threat of new entrants, and threat of substitution, buyer power, and supplier power. Porter (2008) posited that the five forces of competition should be used to determine whether new products and services of organizations have the potential to attain sustainable advantage. Porter emphasized the importance of analyzing the five forces and their effect on a company. This analysis is especially important for entrepreneurs who want to expand their brick-and-mortar business by adding an online element. With qualitative holistic multiple-case design, Yin (2009) conceptualized that academic communities should include theory as part of the design phase of the study.

In describing the theory of competitive rivalry, Porter (2008) indicated that when an entrepreneur moves his or her business online, the number of competitors may increase dramatically, and products that are similar will compete based on price, endangering the new online business' profitability and sustainable advantages. Porter noted that competitive rivalry may affect a business that has many competitors that offer comparable products and services. Although online business opportunities have a larger pool of possible buyers, they also have more competition for market share. Porter (2008) further documented that the factors associated with competitive rivalry are the number of competitors, differences among competitors, customer loyalty, and the cost of leaving the market.

A detailed review of the theory of the threat of new entrants by Porter (1980a, 1980b) indicated that since there is no limit on the number of online business possibilities, there is always the threat of new entrants that can threaten the competitive advantages of established businesses. Porter (1980a, 1980b) argued that brick-and-mortar business are often expensive to start-up so new entrants will be limited, but entry onto the web is relatively inexpensive for a new business. Hence, Porter (1980a, 1980b) theorized that the threat of new entrants is a barrier faced by business owners who want to expand their brick-and-mortar business by adding an online component (Porter, 1980a, 1980b).

With the threat of substitution, Porter (2008) articulated that one of the most overlooked barriers pertains to substitute product. Porter posited that not only must a small business owner know what his or her competitors are selling, he or she must also be aware of what substitute products are available to customers. Porter found that when the cost to consumer is low in switching to a new product the threat of substitute is high. Moreover, Porter demonstrated that marketing managers aggressively price their products when there is a new entry in the industry in an attempt to keep the customer from switching. Porter commented that when the threat of substitutes is high, the profit margin will tend to be low. Finally, Porter determined that the factors associated with threat of substitute product included: (a) the performance of the substitute, (b) the cost of making the change to a substitute, and (c) the cost of switching to a substitute (Porter, 2008).

With the theory of buyer power, Porter (2008) argued that buyer may control the profitability of an online business. Porter (2008) discovered that buyer powers are referred to as the number of buyers, their importance to the business, and switching costs. Businesses that have a few powerful buyers are more likely to control their prices. Porter (2008) found that the factors associated with buyer threat are the number of customers, the size of the order, customer loyalty, and lack of demand from customers.

The last theoretical framework pertains to supplier power. Porter (2008) ascertained that suppliers have the power to force business owners to pay higher prices based on the uniqueness of the products and services. Porter found that businesses that have fewer choices of suppliers are more likely to have competitive advantages. Porter (2008) established that the factors associated with supplier threat are the following: the number of suppliers, the quantity of supplies, the business' ability to substitute, and the cost of the substitution (Porter, 2008).

Saastamoinen (2009) found that sellers are not earning adequate returns on reputation in retail e-commerce. Saastamoinen argued that the evidence depicts that very large sellers (or small sellers) may accrue benefit from their reputations in competition. Saastamoinen discovered that while an increase in the quantity of sellers reduces prices but overall an increase in the quantity of small sellers reduces prices universally (Saastamoinen, 2009).

According to Stambaugh, Yu, and Dubinsky (2011), online managers of SMEs should incorporate strategy before launching competitive attacks. The managers of online SMEs are responsible for formulating clarity, goals, and implementing competitive actions. Stambaugh et al. (2011) argued that the online managers must possess strategic orientations and ensure that their competitive actions are consistent with that orientation, its strategy and its specific strategic outcome.

The current case study was designed to examine the barriers impeding the sustainable advantages for online SMEs in United States. Findings could be used to help other small business owners who may want to expand their customer base by going online. According to Yin (2009), in a qualitative case study, academic communities are known to conduct investigations and data collection by studying several individuals with a common experience. The theoretical proposition in this qualitative holistic multiple-case study was to ascertain whether procedures, risk assessments and business strategies could create sustainable advantages for SMEs that had gone online since 2006. Yin (2003) stated that the use of theory in conducting case study is not only vastly helpful in defining the research design and data collection but also in generalizing the outcome of the case study. This qualitative holistic multiple-case study involved exploring the barriers to online-business profitability for small businesses. During the course of interviews, the participants provided their opinions, inferences, explanation, and online market experiences to inform the current study.

In the current research study, the interview questions were administered in a (respectful, friendly and conversational manner) to enhance the quality, rigor, validity, and diminish misrepresentation (Yin, 2009). To enhance generalizability, the current qualitative holistic multiple-case study pursued the principles for rigor, validity and quality recommended by experienced lecturer like Yin (Yin, 2009). For example, Yin (2009), found that in order to generate higher-quality case study, academic communities should be in compliance with the following strategies: vetting participants before data collection, conducting pilot case study, eradicating biases, inserting interview data into a database, participants

66

acting as informants, reviewing scholarly literature, and participants verifying interview notes of the case study (Yin, 2009).

Participants

Participants were selected for this research using purposeful sampling. A total of 20 participants were selected following purposeful sampling. The purposeful sample in this study included several online small business segments such as technology, home healthcare, education, financial services, legal services, and automobile dealers. In qualitative data collection, academic communities prefer to integrate purposeful sampling to select participants that encountered prior experience pertaining to the phenomenon under study (Zikmund, 2003).

According to Zikmund (2003), purposive sampling is a non-probability sampling method in which a knowledgeable individual selects the sample based on his or her judgment about some appropriate characteristics needed for the sample members. Replications of the case studies are the guiding concept of the research (Yin, 2009). The purpose of this qualitative holistic multiple-case study was to ascertain whether adequate procedures, risk assessment and other prudent strategies could create sustainable advantages for SMEs that had gone online since 2006.

The participants and informants were enlightened regarding the literatures reviewed in the research study. The participants were informed about their protection from sustaining harm, risk, and deception in this case study. The prospective participants were fully informed of no reprisal for their refusal to participate in this case study. The rights to omit questions or withdraw from the study were verbalized to the participants. Compensations were not provided to anyone participating in this research study.

The participants were informed of their voluntary participation in the research project. Participants signed the informed consent forms and confidentiality agreements. The prospective participants were ensured that the information they provided would not be shared, misreported, and disclosed to anyone for any reason. The information from the participants was safeguarded in the locked cabinet and was not revealed to other parties. To comply with ethical code and integrate anonymity, all interview transcripts (deliverables) from the 20 participants were coded, and reviewed solely by individuals in this study. Those coded information were destroyed immediately after the completion of this dissertation.

Materials/Instruments

The question-interview material (Appendix A) was used to gather information to answer the research questions. The goal was to use the instrument to examine barriers impeding sustainable advantages for SMEs. After the participants were chosen, interviews were scheduled. The participants were asked 34 open-ended questions during the interview gathering process of the current research study. In accordance with principles posited by Yin (2009), and Trochim and Donnelly (2007), a pilot case study often pays off in identification of substantial problems with measurement, random, and bias errors before the main study commences.

Professional content assessors often examine the face validity of the interview material. After the review, the professional content assessors are known to approve interview material before the interview instruments are administered to the participants (Zikmund, 2003). In this study, the qualitative data and interview instruments were collected with in-depth interview medium such as face-to-face, telephone, e-mail, and evidence from financial statements of the organizations (Yin, 2009).

The interviews were expected to last approximately 45 minutes. All interviews were tape recorded with the permission of the participants. According to Yin (2009), audiotapes provide verbatim (accurate) rendition of interviews. The interview questions were administered in a respectful, conversational, and unbiased manner (Yin, 2009). This qualitative case study required interactive and in-depth interviews through face-to-face, telephone, and e-mail to ensue rigor (triangulation). All interviews were tape recorded with the permission of the participants. After each interview, the tape recordings were transcribed. At the completion of all interviews, the data collected was entered into a qualitative software program for data analysis. The qualitative software reduced the data to themes that can be reported. A qualitative case study provides an excellent opportunity to comprehend the essence of the experience, viewpoint, and business worldview of the participants (Yin, 2009).

Data Collection, Processing, and Analysis

The current study adopted a qualitative holistic multiple-case design. The qualitative data collection commenced after the Northcentral University Institutional Review Board (IRB) approved the study. To capture the experiences of the participants, interview was conducted with 20 online entrepreneurs by telephone/in person, recorded on audio-tape, and multiple data were inserted into (Excel spreadsheet and case study database) for assessment, to ensure completeness, and accuracy. All the transcripts from the interview were coded (analyzed) by identifying themes as depicted in the tables (Yin, 2009).

A written qualitative investigation interviews were conducted with 20 SMEs owners who had taken their businesses online within the last five years. The research questions were answered by using a qualitative design question-interview material to ask the participants about the barriers impeding the sustainable advantages for SMEs and to ascertain their perspective. In addition, data collection process involved transcribing and preparing the raw information for review (Trochim & Donnelly, 2007; Yin, 2009). In a qualitative case study, data collection procedures are best executed by conducting interviews in a pleasant manner with participants, although documents, observations, and art may also be used (Yin, 2009).

In order to establish construct validity (credibility) in this qualitative case study, the data was collected from diverse online business owners. According to Yin (2009), case study evidence is derivable from multiple sources of evidence such as: documents, archival records, interviews, direct observation, participation, and physical artifacts (Yin, 2009). The current research study enhanced credibility by including multiple sources of evidence, chain of evidence, and allowed key informants to cross check draft case study report (Yin, 2009). The most imperative advantage provided by using multiple sources of evidence was the integration of converging line of inquiry, completeness, triangulation, convincing finding, and accurate conclusion in a case study (Yin, 2009). During the data analysis phase of dissertation, the following Yin principles such as: internal validity, pattern matching, explanation building, vetting rival explanation, and logic methods were addressed (Yin, 2009). In order to comply with the rigor of reliability, all data collected were embedded into a case study database (Yin, 2009).

In order to ensure validity and reliability, a panel of three professors was enlisted to comment on the interview questions. Immediately after IRB approval, a pilot test of the interview questions were conducted with two business owners to ensure that the questions elicit the type of information necessary to understand the barriers to sustainable advantages faced by online SMEs in United States. There was no outstanding ambiguity or error to be amended in the interview questions. In all case studies, Yin (2009) stated that academic communities should integrate credibility, trustworthiness, confirmability, and data dependability in order to integrate the quality, and authenticity of qualitative research as a methodology. In a qualitative case study, the academicians can conduct data analysis strategies by analyzing data for imperative statements, holistic attributes, and meaningful attributes of real-life events, textural description, structural description, and description of the essence (Yin, 2003; Yin 2009).

This study explored the barriers to sustainable advantages among owners of online small businesses. Therefore, academic communities may incur difficulty in generalizing the findings to online organizations conducting business on a global scale. This study excluded organizations that conduct online businesses on a global scale. The findings were often limited due to lack of access to primary and secondary data required to explore the barriers impeding sustainable advantages for SMEs in United States. According to Trochim and Donnelly (2007), academic communities may employ unobtrusive measurement to mitigate the biases that ensue from the intrusion of the measurement instrument. Some academicians use indirect measures, content analysis, and secondary analysis to conduct unobtrusive measurement.

The analytical strategies used in this current study were pattern matching, rival explanations, and theoretical propositions. In a qualitative holistic multiple-case study, Yin (2009) established that theory is imperative for conducting data collection, processing, and analysis. Data analysis can be described as examining, categorizing, tabulating, and testing to answer the research questions of the case study (Yin, 2009). In data analysis, academic individual might recombine quantitative (or qualitative) evidence to resolve the research problem of the case study (Yin, 2009). Any of these techniques can be used in practicing five methods for analyzing case studies: pattern matching, explanation building, logic models, and cross-case synthesis (Yin, 2003; Yin, 2009). The pattern matching, explanation building, and logic models can be used to analyze data, whether the academic communities are conducting a multiple-case or a single case design (Yin, 2009). Reliability of the findings were ensured by having participants evaluate their own transcribed interviews to ascertain that the transcripts accurately reflected what the participants articulated in the current research study (Yin, 2009). In this research, a qualitative software program, Nvivo 8, was used to analyze each participant's interview transcript and the data from the interviews were developed into cogent findings, and recommendations (Yin, 2009).

Methodological Assumptions, Limitations, and Delimitations

The methodological assumptions contained evidence that entrepreneurs that emanated from the online SMEs were prospective research participants. The participants were regarded as truthful, credible, dependable, and honest in the current study (Yin, 2003). The findings from this study relied on truthful representations of the participants and the interpretation of everybody involved. The results of qualitative case study would be authentic when the participants are trustworthy (Yin, 2009).

The participants of the current study had experiences (or complete knowledge) of the barriers confronting the sustainable advantages of SMEs in online markets. The research participants may choose to answer the open-ended questions honestly and voluntarily; otherwise, the validity of the findings would be limited (Yin, 2003; Yin, 2009). The data that emanated from interviews were conversational thereby limiting scope of this study to focus on exploring the barriers which may impede the sustainable advantages for SMEs in online markets. Therefore, academic communities may incur difficulty in generalizing the findings from this research to online organizations that operate on a global scale. Another limitation was that this study excluded organizations conducting online businesses on a global scale (Yin, 2003; Yin, 2009).

Ethical Assurances

The participants were apprised of the intent of the study. Using a signed informed consent form, the participants were acquainted with the code of honesty with professional colleagues and their protection from harm. As part of compliance with the ethical standard, the research participants were informed about their right to privacy, confidentiality, informed consent, and adequate protection of their information. To comply with ethical code, and integrate anonymity, academic communities always use coding, and recording strategies to eliminate the names of the participants (Yin, 2009). The approval of IRB was obtained before the commencement of data collection for this dissertation.

The interview questions did not include the names or identity of the participants in order to preserve their confidentiality, privacy, anonymity, and ethical assurances (Yin, 2009). The information from the participants was safeguarded in a locked cabinet and was not disclosed to other parties (or competitors). Those coded information and interview notes were destroyed immediately after the completion of this dissertation. This study was conducted with consistent and effective two-way communication with participants. All information collected (or analyzed) in this study was held at the highest level of confidentiality and was destroyed immediately after the completion of this research study.

The ethical issue of honesty with professional colleagues was attained by providing honest and authentic information on all required forms. The participants and everybody involved in the current research study followed the benchmark of truthful interpretation pertaining to interview transcripts. The prospective participants were ensured that the data they provided would not be shared, misrepresented, misreported, and disclosed to anyone for any reason. Deception occurs when participants perceive that the study has one purpose but the interviewer has a different one (Yin, 2009).

The ethical issue of right to privacy was administered by not including personal dossier of the participants. All participants were assigned pseudonyms or alphabetized coding such as (1), (2), (3) to honor their privacy and these pseudonyms were used in all verbal communication and written records of the current research study. The participants were informed of their voluntary participation in the current research study. Compensations were not provided to anyone participating in this research study. The participants were informed about their protection from sustaining physical harm, emotional harm, and coercion in this research. The prospective participants were fully informed of no reprisal for their refusal to participate in this case study and their rights to omit question(s) or withdraw from the study.

When research involves human beings, the potential ethical issue may occur, in this study, loss of confidentiality was a prospective ethical issue. Participants were assured that the name of the company and their names, geographic locations, dossier and content of the interviews would not be shared or disclosed to anyone for any reason. Anonymity of participants' deliverable, such as (name of the company/participant, notes, audio tapes, data and deliverables) transliterated in the current study was maintained by alphabet coding of participants (such as, case participant (1); case participant (2); and case participant (3). All participants were protected from undesirable and debilitating circumstances (Yin, 2009).

Summary

This qualitative holistic multiple-case study explored the barriers impeding the online business sustainable advantages for SMEs in online markets. In a qualitative case study, the academic communities are known to use instrument to collect the experiences, viewpoint, practices, and interpretations from the participants (Trochim & Donnelly, 2007). In a qualitative case study, the academic communities are incorporating key informants or company gatekeepers to describe the experiences and viewpoints (Creswell, 2007; Yin, 2009).

The theoretical proposition in this qualitative holistic multiple-case study was to ascertain whether internal control and business strategies could create sustainable advantages for SMEs that had gone online since 2006. According to Yin (2009), in a qualitative case study, academic communities are known to conduct investigations and data collection by studying several individuals with a common experience. Multiple sources of evidence were reviewed and analyzed together, so that the case study's finding were based on the convergence of data from diverse online entrepreneurs (Creswell, 2007; Yin, 2009).

Chapter 4

The purpose of this qualitative holistic multiple-case study was to explore the procedures and risk assessment in use for eliminating the aggressive rivalry of sellers, which may impede the sustainable advantages for SMEs which had gone online since 2006. The lived experiences of the participants informed the online small business owners on how to optimize profit and the importance of eradicating barriers to sustainable advantages for SMEs in online marketplaces. The purpose was to understand the experience from each participant's viewpoint, opinions, practices, point of view and experiences. The qualitative design for this research was a qualitative holistic multiple-case study. Toward that goal, the purpose of this study was to provide an explanation and meaning about the barriers to online-business profitability for small businesses in United States.

During the data collection process, 20 participants responded to the invitation to participate in this study. Twenty entrepreneurs who had taken their businesses online within the last five years were interviewed to determine what barriers they faced in achieving sustainable advantages (or profitability) for SMEs in online marketplaces. The supporting interview questions were created directly from the primary research questions (see Appendix A). The primary research questions with supporting interview questions were administered to all participants. All the participants contributed data to address the research questions and infused validity to the current research study.

In order to maintain rigor, potential biases were mitigated (Yin, 2009). To overcome any potential biases, and to enhance generalizability, the participants re-verified and endorsed the draft interview report, findings, interpretations and the draft report. The implications of the data were scrutinized by three members of doctoral committee. The feedback of committee members and the participants were incorporated into the final report (Yin, 2009). This descriptive qualitative data was collected using interviews with small business owners in the United States regions and the study added value to the literature.

The following research questions were developed for this study:

Q1: What procedures, methods and risk assessments are used to eliminate barriers to online-business sustainable advantages for small business?

Q2: How are the procedures, methods and risk assessments implemented?

Q3: How are procedures, methods and risk assessments monitored and verified?

Q4: What are the key problems connected with implementing the procedures, methods and risk assessments to eliminate barriers?

Q5: What primary internal controls (manuals or flow-charts) are used to eradicate barriers?

Q6: What profitability models and/or methods do online small businesses use to generate income?

Research questions 1 through 6 findings were derived from interviews with 20 online small business owners. The findings of the current case study were presented in the results section.

Results

The participants were selected after the Northcentral University Institutional Review Board (IRB) approved the study. The population for the current qualitative holistic multiple-case study consisted of 20 entrepreneurs who had taken their businesses online since 2006. Participants were selected for this research using purposeful sampling. The names of the online small business owners (participants) were obtained from the United States Chamber of Commerce. Qualitative strategies were used to explore barriers to sustainable advantages for SMEs which had gone online since 2006.

The multiple-case sample in the current study represented online small business segments such as technology, home healthcare, education, financial services, legal services, and automobile dealers. The participants were interviewed during the months of November 2011 through January 2012. The qualitative

77

data were collected using in-depth interviews with 20 online entrepreneurs who within the last five years had expanded their brick and mortar businesses to an online storefront.

The purpose of this qualitative holistic multiple-case study was to ascertain whether adequate procedures, risk assessment and business strategies created sustainable advantages for SMEs that had gone online since 2006. Twenty entrepreneurs (adults over the age of 18) who had taken their businesses online within the last five years were interviewed. After the participants were chosen, 45-minute interviews were conducted. The participants were asked 34 open-ended interview questions relating specifically to the primary research questions. Participants were instructed to respond to the interview questions based on their viewpoints, experience, opinions, practices, and beliefs.

This qualitative holistic multiple-case study adhered to Yin case study principle of collecting and documenting chains of evidence to enhance the quality of this dissertation. The data collected from the participants were documented in a case study database and Microsoft Word to attain reliability of the study. Multiple viewpoints and experiences from different online small business segments (20 small business owners) provided different sources and enough data to triangulate the findings (Yin, 2009).

The 20 online small business owners informed the current study by providing the following: (a) convergence answers, (b) divergence responses, (c) corroboration, (d) multiple sources of evidences, and (e) chain of evidence. The participants provided data that were rigorously perused and compared to other existing studies. Yin case study principles provided imperative scholarships for conducting high-quality multiple-case studies (Yin, 2009). The participants provided imperative insight about whether adequate procedures, risk assessments,

78

and business strategies created sustainable advantages for SMEs in online environment.

The interview instruments were used to collect (viewpoints, opinions, practices and experiences) of the participants regarding the research topic. The participants were asked to re-verify and endorse the deliverable from the data of interviews. All interviews were tape-recorded with the permission of the participants. Participants were informed that audio recordings and field notes collected in the current research study would be safeguarded in a locked cabinet, and destroyed immediately after the completion of this research study. After each interview, the audio recordings were transcribed. At the completion of all interviews, the data collected were entered into a qualitative software program for data analysis.

In accordance with the qualitative holistic multiple-case study design, a pilot test was conducted on the instrument (interview questions) in order to develop relevant lines of questions. After IRB approval, a pilot test of the interview questions were conducted with two business owners to ensure that the questions elicit the type of information necessary to understand the barriers that may prevent sustainable advantages for SMEs in online environment. Two entrepreneurs participated in the pilot study, one from personal computer retail, and the other from cell phone retail organization.

After the pilot test participants were chosen, 45-minute interviews were scheduled. The pilot test interview took place at the office of the two knowledgeable business owners who are citizens of United States. During the pilot test interview, the two business owners were asked to review and sign the informed consent form. To capture the entire information, all interviews were tape-recorded with the permission of the pilot study participants. The participants were asked 34 open-ended interview questions and the participants also evaluated the pilot test (interview notes) for ambiguity or error. At the completion of all interviews and review of information, the pilot test (or interview notes) did not reveal finding, ambiguity, and error in the interview questions.

The results from the present qualitative holistic multiple-case study were reported in this chapter and chapter 5. Additional data presented in chapter 4 included the major themes that were developed from the primary research questions, supporting interview questions and responses derived from 20 participants. In addition, the chapter consisted of a description of the nodes that were used to develop the themes.

Themes

Twenty participants responded to the invitation to participate in this case study. All participants were asked the primary research questions and supporting interview questions. The participants contributed their experience, viewpoint, skills, and meaning, to the research study. The in-depth personal interviews were conducted at the scheduled locations. The interviews data was recorded, organized, perused and reviewed. Once all interviews were completed, the data were entered in NVivo 8.

The data were then sorted by frequencies of words or phrases used. The software allowed all individuals to explore trends, find meanings, and identify emerging themes. The terms that were used to develop the themes include website navigation problems, customer with no computers, no repeat purchases, lack of personal interaction, lack of computer literacy, and insufficient web traffic.

After sorting, the data were placed under one of the major three themes: barriers to the operation of an online business, strategies used to mitigate those barriers, and methods that were utilized to maximize profit. The following section describes each theme and provides the participants responses. In this chapter and the next, many of the themes were analyzed and compared to previous findings from the literature.

After all the sorting was completed, the data were placed under one of the major three themes that emerged regarding the study. The first theme was barriers to the operation of an online business. The second theme was strategies used to mitigate those barriers. The third theme was methods that were utilized to maximize profit. The following section includes a detailed description of each theme with responses given from participants. In this chapter and the next, many of the themes were evaluated and compared to previous findings from the literature.

Research Findings from Question 1 -Theme 1: Barriers to the operation of an online business. What procedures, methods and risk assessments are used to eliminate barriers to online-business sustainable advantages for small business? When participants were queried on research question and supporting interview questions, nearly all of the participants indicated in the interviews that they had experienced lack of repeat purchase from the online customers. The participants also noted that they had no way of registering customers' complaints, eliciting customer opinions or feedback, and using them to encourage repeat purchases. Most participants claimed that their managers were reluctant to be proactive in order to make their company more competitive.

Seven of the participants made interesting point that their main problem was funding, but two participants indicated that an occasional face-to-face interaction with prospective customers could add to their online sales. Participants 5, 6, and 8 made the same comment about lack of communication. The participants were probed on procedures, methods, and risk assessment used to eliminate barriers five participants commented on their board membership, and banking industry experience. Participants also offered histories of their online companies. They also noted that they had not been able to obtain business loans. The participants were determined to secure loans for their online companies.

The participants remarked that their online organization could not monitor products or their customers' service preferences. Skype and GoToMeeting could be used to encourage customers to take and enthusiasm survey. The entrepreneurs could then use the feedback to respond to the needs and demands of their customers. Several participants supported the business model of conducting community outreach programs and presentations and publishing newsletters to counter ineffective marketing programs. One participant explained that customer calls and inquiries were not answered promptly. This participant suggested that that customer service departments respond to customer calls in one or two hours.

Almost half of the participants reported that the lack of face-to-face contact was a problem. According to one participant, "For business people who had become accustomed to dealing with customer in-person, the challenge of rethinking how to deal with the unseen customer was a significant challenge." Another participant complained of "the impossibility of meeting or seeing the client face-to-face." The third participant denoted the "impossibility of answering immediate questions of customers." Seven participants expressed their views on the difficulty of keeping customers. They claim that online shoppers were not as loyal as shoppers at brick-and-mortar stores. Thus, the owners thought that encouraging repeat business was one of their most serious problems.

Business owners held their employees accountable for ensuring the safety, protection and security of customer information on the web site. Keeping customer information safe and secure is essential to the success of online business. Three of the participants stated that their managers could not afford to hire in-house auditors. Nor did the online managers perform risk assessment. The participants added that they have not been able to convince their online customers that their information would be safe.

The participants mentioned that managers did not anticipate that easy to navigate website would raise the company's bottom line. They also cited inefficiencies affecting the ease of website navigation. According to some participants, there online managers did not take advantage of the online tools for customers. A few participants asserted that their managers did not provide website improvement and sustainability. Five participants admitted their websites were not up to date. Three participants said that their websites did not contain the right information.

Research Findings from Questions 2 and 3 - Theme 2: Strategies implemented to mitigate barriers. How are the procedures, methods and risk assessments implemented? How are procedures, methods and risk assessments monitored and verified? The participants believed that their prospective customers either do not own a computer or do not have Internet access. Some participants also claimed that the vast majority of people are not computer literate. Business owners were not aware that prospective customers needed mentorship and outreach from online businesses to provide free computer and educational programs. Thus, business owners had to make sure that their customers had computers and Internet access.

Participants 16, 17, 18, 19 and 20 indicated that use of debit cards online would only lead to fraud and identity theft. The remaining participants included the problem of thin margin affecting online products and inadequate number of buyers needed to make profit. Most of the participants had corporate offices.

Participants stated that the online customers were not invited to visit the office in order to embolden relationship between consumers and organization leaders. Some participants asserted that they had customer service representatives available by telephone and email, and open online forums for their customers.

Business owners did not offer discounts to their online customers. Some participants noted the problems of late delivery of products. One participant responded that the method implemented was online-sales support but in order to build relationship, the organizational leaders did not invite customers to the offline office due to insurance liability. Several participants stated that they did not understand why the management had not implemented appreciation days, scholarships, gifts, and discounts to attract online customers.

A few participants stated that investing in state-of-the-art online security software would qualify as a potent strategy for mitigating barriers. Other participants believed that online managers should mitigate barriers by keeping graphic user (interface) simple and user friendly. Some participants commented that managers in their company did not hire personnel to monitor website publication, manage website navigation, and reduce sustainability barriers. To mitigate barriers, other participants recommended that sending sales personnel to neighborhoods to tell people how to buy cheap products on the Internet. Some participants did not understand why the managers in the organization had not written a policy instructing stakeholders (employees) to invite people to use free computer at the local library or in their local offline office. Even the business owners did not implement the strategy of offering free computer classes to people in their corporate offices.

When the participants were asked to converse about the strategies implemented to mitigate barriers, the responses were substantive. For example, several participants stated that the prospective consumers were not invited to visit the offline location. Business owners were indirectly losing prospective customers because they failed to administered strategies to mitigate barriers. Another participant explained that customers' service representatives were not required to tutor computer illiterate individuals on Internet navigation.

To curb fraud and other anomalies, participants stated that the policies and procedures of the company were embedded on the web sites discouraging customers to use debit card online; they are free to use Master or Visa credit cards to make their payments. Another participant stated that the organizational managers requested consumers to call the web site telephone number in order to log complaints on fraud. Accordingly, some participants stated that the necessary steps were taken to inform the customers about the protection of their personal dossier, credit cards, and that the website and servers are safeguarded with firewall (or McAfee) software.

The participants noted the problem of thin margin affecting online products and inadequate number of buyers needed to make profit. The participants indicated that business owners should focus on the strategies of concentrating on higher volume of sales or economies of scale. In addition, business owners should embark upon massive advertisement. For example, to combat competition, participant 19 stated that "We advertise and promote the brand of the organization." The participants emphasized that online small business owners should sell the products the competitors are not proffering to the consumers. One participant said that the business owners should refuse to go into markets that are not presently lucrative.

A few participants stated that the strategies implemented by the business owners were not effective to mitigate barriers because business owners failed to review the anomalies, determine their cause, and correct them. The managers should implement additional controls that are necessary to mitigate those barriers. According to some participants, several customers do not own personal computers. Further, the participants said that the government did not invest enough funds in computer producing industries to make the price of computer component affordable for potential consumers. One participant stated the business owner cannot boast of repeat sales and retention of the customers. Participant 20 articulated, "The strategies are enough to mitigate the impact on our products due to the physical barriers we are experiencing in the market. No doubt they will be effective on the short run while giving us time to establish our presence in the market and make long range plans."

Research Findings from Questions 4 and 5: What are the key problems connected with implementing the procedures, methods and risk assessments to eliminate barriers? What primary internal controls (manuals or flow-charts) are used to eradicate barriers? When participants were queried on research questions 4 and 5 and supporting interview questions, participants asserted that many organizations could not implement their procedures due to inadequate knowledge of competitors' plans, lack of strategies, and financial shortages. The participants noted that most entrepreneurs were ignorant of the kind of jeopardy imposed upon business by barriers; neither had they any business knowledge of how/when to implement solution to manage risks and barriers.

Most participants interviewed commented that many organizations suffered from lost opportunities, failure and lack of progress in their business. Several participants asserted that these problems were further compounded by the fact that the small business owners could not find think tanks with sufficient insights to address these barriers. Almost all participants concluded that the academic communities should take the burden to write papers highlighting peculiar barriers and proffering technical based solutions to counter barriers.

Most participants stated the organizations did not incorporate internal control manuals (or flow-charts) to eradicate barriers due to lack of information, insufficient knowledge, inadequate experience, cost, and other reasons. Participants asserted that the business owners should diligently read through and understand auditing technical principles pertaining to preventing barriers. Auditing concepts could help organizational leaders to create and implement internal control manuals (or flow-charts) that may be used to eradicate barriers. Almost all participants enumerated that without internal control manuals (or flow-charts), organizations would not be equipped to wage an effective intelligent and result-oriented war on forces of barriers affecting sustainable advantages. Almost all participants agreed that the organizational managers were not confident enough to develop standard internal control manuals and flow charts for the company. The leaders did not train employees on the principle of eradicating barriers.

From the participants' perspective, the internal control manuals (or flow-charts) had not been developed for key areas pertinent to eradicate barriers. Participants commented that they preferred internal controls to help eliminate barriers in order to achieve the mission and objectives of organizations. The participants indicated that the responsible management in their organization did not have a viable written monitoring, and verification policy to eliminate barriers. Most participants conceded that their organizations did not believe in the concept of risk prevention.

Research Findings from Question 6 -Theme 3: Methods used to maximize profit. What profitability models and/or methods do online small businesses use to generate income? When participants were queried on research question 6 and supporting interview questions, the responses were colossal; most participants cited the use of economic of scale to maximize profits. Business owners instituted economies of scale to increase total number of student admissions to the school. The business owners believed that the more students admitted to the school, the less the cost per student, and the higher the profitability. The business owners updated their methods to elicit big retention. The efforts of the business owners were tied to maximization of student enrollment. The business owners engaged massively in advertisement to maximize profit. Most participants emphasized that online managers did not create policy and procedure on repeat purchase and customer retention. Some participants did not understand why the managers in their organization refused to embed policy for repeat purchase, and customer retention on the company database or intranet.

To maximize profit, the participants cited the following methods: online marketing models, market structure, advertisement models, and market share. Another method cited by the business owners were advertisement on search engine, television, and web site. According to narratives of several participants, additional methods documented to maximize profit were door to door advertisement, online marketing, powerful website, exit splash, and YouTube. Some participants stated that the online managers invited their customers to visit the ground location in order to repair their cell phones.

To maximize profit, other business owners were comfortable with the methods regarded as economic of scale, twitter, using exit splash software, and YouTube marketing. Other participants stated that the business owners preferred to use search engine optimization, and free advertisement available on the Internet. Some responding participants indicated that their online businesses sustained competition from large businesses with more capital, and name recognition. A few participants noted that their organizations did not receive adequate number of buyers needed to make profit and lacked sufficient visitors to the websites.

The analysis of the data from the interview indicated that the business owners had different processes to maximize profit. The participants asserted that business owners did not extend product discounts to influence consumers to purchase products. Early in the interview sessions, the participants emphasized that the business owners were oriented in using sponsorships models, marketing models, and benefit participations models to maximize profit. The participants interviewed were of the opinion that the business owners maintain modest advertising budget and incorporated the following: print media in entertainment book, Online Links, memorable brand, online marketing, Facebook commerce, and search engine optimization blog. Small-business owners believed blogging provides value for marketing business, however, some participants stated that small-business owners did not believe online coupon could boost the numbers of shoppers that would navigate, and purchase on their websites.

Many participants stated that the business owners were not advertising with flyers posters, community-banner, celebrity support, business card, and billboard. To expose the brand to consumers, some participants stated that managers prefer to use blogging marketing, Facebook commerce, online marketing, YouTube and discussion on open forums. The online organizations are embracing YouTube, Facebook commerce, and iPad to develop relationships, transparency, and mutual benefits with consumers. These powerful technological tools could help organizations achieve their anticipated financial goals.

All participants reported using methods like Facebook commerce, online marketing, YouTube, open forums, search help desk, product support, Twitter, Flickr from Yahoo, and Atomic blogging to maximize profit. The participants stated that online managers were implementing the company presence in popular search engines to maximize profit. During the interview, the participants informed the study that business owners were using website help to generate leads of potential customers. Some participants stated that leaders were providing information about the products to targeted customer base. Several participants stated that SMEs are incorporating Google search engine, Yahoo search engines, networking with other organizations, membership in business referral groups, and customer referral networking groups. The participants cited that online sales group had the ability to expedite action on online traffic.

During the fieldwork of the study it was determined that small business owners had their own unique methods to maximize profit. For example, participant 2, 4 and 7 stated that from their experience as business administrator, in order to maximize profit the managers prefer cost effectiveness, cost control, and proactive marketing approach. However, other participants revealed that some managers do it differently; for example, to maximize profit, the online managers prefer to cut expenses, keep cost low, and increase sales by selling quality products.

To maximize profit, ten of the 20 participants mentioned that business owners advertise with Twitter, banner advertising, MySpace, Blogging, and social networking. Another participant said that organizational leaders did not have foresight to grant free computers gifts to prospective customers to boost sales and traffic on their web sites. Finally, to maximize profit, the participants reflected that several online business owners required their workforce to generate higher volume of sales. The participants identified that to increase profit;

most online business owner promoted online visibility with Google as their provider. The participants interviewed were of the opinion that the business owners instituted effective profitability models. A few participants believed that e-commerce organizations had become very popular in their community. The business owners believed that the profitability models established in their organizations were effective, and most likely to succeed.

Participants stated that the profitability models established can be deemed responsible for lot of sales and revenue. In brief, participant 16 stated "We are getting a higher volume of sales. We are getting more prospective customers to know and visit our site blame this on the profitability models established by the management." As part of the discussion of the effectiveness of profitability models, the participants informed this study that each business owners had their own preference for profitability model. Participants also indicated that the more money expended to increase awareness to the public, the more enrollments would manifest for the business owners. Most managers prefer advertisements such as television adverts, internet, blogs, YouTube, and popular newspaper advertisement. Some participants explicated that the managers should use effective advertisement to expose the brand to the consumers. Many participants concluded that television seems more popular but is very expensive.

Some participants elucidated that the organization management did not capture the identity of their competitors to record on Microsoft database. A few participants claimed that the managers did not maintain road maps to eliminate impending threat of substitute products that could threaten the sustainable advantages (profit) of their company. Another participant stated that business owners should make customers acknowledge that the organization offer superior products. One participant claimed that management and stakeholders did not brainstorm or plan to reduce financial loss imminent from power of the consumers that drives down the price of the products or services. Participants reported that business owners should form a partnership with several suppliers in order to pay lower prices to stakeholders, and suppliers.

Evaluation of Findings

The purpose of this qualitative holistic multiple-case study was to ascertain whether business owners created sustainable advantages for SMEs in online markets. The motivation for this research was to contribute and disseminate imperative knowledge about exploring the barriers to profitability of online businesses for small businesses in the United States. In short, exploring the barriers to profitability of online businesses for small business was an exemplary as well as a brand new study in the academic communities. The qualitative data was collected using in-depth interviews through face-to-face interviews, follow up telephone interviews, and e-mail interviews with 20 small business owners. To enhance generalizability, the participants re-verified and endorsed the findings as the barriers to sustainable advantages for SMEs online business operations.

This research asked: Research question 1: What procedures, methods and risk assessments are used to eliminate barriers to online-business sustainable advantages for small business? Research question 2: How are the procedures, methods and risk assessments implemented? Research question 3: How are procedures, methods and risk assessments monitored and verified? Research question 4: What are the key problems connected with implementing the procedures, methods and risk assessments to eliminate barriers? Research question 5: What primary internal controls (manuals or flow-charts) are used to eradicate barriers? Research question 6: What profitability models and/or methods do online small businesses use to generate income? The participants reviewed the themes that emerged, and confirmed the accuracy of the verbiage (or interpretations).

Evaluation of findings for research question 1. What procedures, methods and risk assessments are used to eliminate barriers to online-business sustainable advantages for small business? In response to this question, seven participants commented that funding was the greatest problem, but two claimed that an occasional face-to-face interaction with prospective customers could increase online sales. Three more participants made the same comment about the problem of lack of communication. These remarks reinforced the findings of Durand (2006), Aziz and Poorsartep (2009), and Doherty and Lockett (2007), who argued that the lack of face-to-face contact with the customers often undermined customer loyalty. To solve this problem, managers are now taking advantage of online video conferencing technology.

Ratnasingam (2008), and Karakaya and Stahl (2009) identified that interaction with customers often generate revenue for businesses. Gardner (2007), Chong (2008), and Doherty and Lockett (2007) also agreed that the factor affecting e-commerce resources included lack of technical expertise, interaction, lack of funding, and the steep learning curve that e-commerce demands. The business owners should know that policy (or internal controls) is a defense even as risk assessment is a defense that shields and preserves organizations from debilitating powers of barriers. O'Dwyer and Ledwith (2009), Karakaya and Stahl (2009), and Wong (2007) showed that capital prerequisite influences the competitive advantages and the sustainability of rival firms. Stambaugh et al. (2011), Suki et al. (2008), and Beaver (2007) declared that organizations with vast financial funding enjoy long-term competitive advantages.

93

Rickards (2007), Smith (2005), and Wong (2007) maintained that capital prerequisites influence organizational performance.

Online entrepreneurs should improve their customer services. Customers should not be treated in a condescending manner and should never be kept waiting to receive feedback. When customers approach an employee with a question or complaint, the employee must give the matter immediate attention. Small business owners should be particularly courteous and thoughtful when communicating over e-mail, blog, or telephone. Dikolli and Sedatole (2007), Burgess and Tatnall (2007), and Beaver (2007) asserted that when consumers are satisfied with interaction, from a company, then they will buy its products and services.

Bharadwaj and Soni (2007), Gardner (2007), and Yan (2007) reported that accurate market information is vital to profitability. SME owners should establish timely and truthful marketing communication. Online small business owners should use relationship building interactions to generate demand from customers. The entrepreneurs in this study reinforced the findings of Smolander and Rossi (2008), Aziz and Poorsartep (2009), and Chong (2008), who concluded that when management incorporates legacy or slow systems into new e-business functionality, profitability suffers. Rickards (2007), Smith (2005), and Wong (2007) asserted that upper management and managers are responsible for maintaining security protocol and protection of the dossiers pertaining to the customers and stakeholders.

Evaluation of findings for research questions 2 and 3. How are the procedures, methods and risk assessments implemented? How are procedures, methods and risk assessments monitored and verified? Offstein and Childers (2008), Vachon (2011), and Xu et al. (2007) concluded that governments or private entities are investing in research and development to reduce the cost of personal computers. Guerrero et al. (2007), Beck and Franke (2008), and Burgess and Tatnall (2007), recommended that entrepreneurs learn to accommodate, train, support, and assist consumers with less computer experience.

Participants added the company telephone numbers to their web sites to respond to emergencies or inquiries. The participants in this study validated the finding of Dikolli and Sedatole (2007), Darbyshire (2008), and Auger (2005), who found that organizations are integrating value-added services such as online parcel tracking, customer care, 24 hours telephone services and delivery notification. Some participants commented that they had no personnel to monitor website publication, website navigation, and solve website navigation problems. The findings from this study differ for those of Karakaya and Stahl (2009), Durand (2006), and Beaver (2007) which concluded that online managers should add these job functions.

The findings in this study corroborate Porter (1998 and 2008). Porter (1998 and 2008) found that the higher the threat of substitutes, the lower the profit margin of small businesses. Porter concluded that small business owners are eradicating the threats of substitute products and thin margins. Dikolli and Sedatole (2007), Doherty and Lockett (2007), and Burgess and Tatnall (2007) emphasized that business owners must protect the data of their consumers. Dembla et al. (2007), Beaver (2007), and Beck and Franke (2008) asserted that entrepreneurs would derive sustainable advantages by integrating customer support, relationships, offline locations and customer service representatives to maximize their customer base, and minimize transaction costs. This finding in this study did not support Dembla et al. (2007), Beaver (2007), and Beck and Franke (2008) findings.

Garrity et al. (2007), and Darbyshire (2008), Suki et al. (2008), and Durand (2006) emphasized that business owners are incorporating strategies to understand customer expectations, quick delivery of orders, resolve problems, and satisfy customers. To mitigate barriers, the participants commented about the availability of customer service, product support, and online forums on the web sites of their company. The remaining findings did not support those of Garrity et al. (2007), and Darbyshire (2008), Suki et al. (2008), and Durand (2006).

Guerrero et al. (2007), Wong (2007), and Repchuck (2008) found that several online managers are using virus software on their network to elicit website security, reliability, user satisfaction, easy navigation and consumer satisfaction. The findings in this study authenticate Guerrero et al. (2007), Wong (2007), and Repchuck (2008) findings. A few participants stated that investing in state-of-the-art online security software would remove barriers. Other participants believed that online managers should keep the graphic user interface simple and user friendly.

In contrast, Rauyruen et al. (2009), Karakaya and Stahl (2009), and Palvia and D'Aubeterre (2007) found that online managers should add webmasters. In contrast, Hettche and Walker (2010), Doherty and Lockett (2007), and Dikolli and Sedatole (2007) reported that business owners are attaining reward because of their extensive relationship with the prospective and current customers. The innovative business owners are committed to implementing more oversight to help eradicate barrier and growth challenges.

Accordingly, some participants stated that the managers provided online free software to the customers for protecting personal dossier, identity, and credit cards. To protect the consumers, the online managers use anti-virus software and firewalls. Arcand et al. (2007),

Khattab et al. (2010), and Loghry and Veach (2009) emphasized that the managers have fiduciary responsibility to protect the consumers and to conduct an annual or quarterly risk assessment.

The participants indicated that business owners should concentrate on higher sales or economies of scale. In addition, business owners should advertise aggressively. The participants emphasized that small business owners should sell the products that their competitors do not offer. One participant said that the business owners should avoid markets that are not lucrative. Hodges and Kent (2007), Meroño-Cerdán (2008), and Ratnasingam (2008) found that several organizations are embarking on revenue models such as: product quality, sales accumulation, customer growth, online advertisement models, and cost effectiveness to maximize profit. According to Porter (2008), the managers are attaining customer loyalty, distinguishing products, continuous improvement, and customization of products to achieve sustainable advantages.

Evaluation of findings for research questions 4 and 5. What are the key problems connected with implementing the procedures, methods and risk assessments to eliminate barriers? What primary internal controls are used to eradicate barriers? Several participants asserted that these problems were compounded by the fact that the online business owners could not find think tanks with sufficient insights to address these barriers. The participants contradicted the findings of Gardner (2007), and Audretsch and Lehmann (2006), who argued that many entrepreneurs benefit from the knowledge of competitive advantages from seminars, chamber of commerce, internal auditors, and certified public accountants. Chong and Pervan (2007) concluded that the fear of losing customers and market share expedites organizational learning.

Wong (2007), Smith (2005), and Rickards (2007) demonstrated that some entrepreneurs know how to compete. The force of competition is detrimental to the market value and financial well-being of any organization. The participants contradicted Loghry and Veach (2009), Chong (2008), and Darbyshire (2008), who stated that business owners are learning from online forums, networks, business, and marketing associations. The participants noted that most owners of SMEs did not know when or how to manage risks and barriers. Rickards (2007), Smith (2005), and Wong (2007) recommended that entrepreneurs leverage the experience of the managers and stakeholders to gain a competitive edge.

From the participants' perspective, the internal control manuals had not been developed for key areas. The participants challenged Simpson et al. (2006), Antlova (2009), and Chong (2008), who asserted that policies are used by business owners to identify the strengths of the internal controls and attain business objectives. Participants preferred internal control. They validated the finding of Darbyshire (2008), Gardner (2007), and Hong (2007), who stated that business owners should have clear internal control policies and managers to enforce them. Ratnasingam (2008), Malaga (2007), and Saastamoinen (2009) found that entrepreneurs had understood the scope of potential risks.

The participants indicated that the responsible management in their organization did not have a viable written monitoring, and verification policy to eliminate barriers. Most participants conceded that their organizations did not believe in the concept of risk prevention. The participants contradicted Yan (2007), Gardner (2007), and Galloway and Mochrie (2005), who emphasized that the entrepreneurs should have internal control policies. Data on risks should be accumulated in preparation for the formal review.

Evaluation of findings for research question 6. What profitability models and/or methods do online small businesses use to generate income? Some participants stated that business owners prefer advertising on blogs and search engines. Some participants did not understand why their managers in their organization refused to embed policy for repeat purchase and customer retention on the company database or intranet. Quinton and Mohammed (2009), Rauyruen et al. (2009), and Wong (2007) concluded that organizational managers that train personnel in customer relations often benefit from customer retention and higher profits.

The participants stated that business owners are using Facebook commerce, online marketing, YouTube, open forums, search help desk, product support, Flickr, and Atomic blogging to maximize profit. The participants stated that online managers are creating a company presence on popular search engines to maximize profit. The online sales group had the ability to drive online traffic. The participants claimed to use websites to generate leads by providing product information to a targeted customer base. Several participants stated that SMEs are incorporating Google search engine, Yahoo search engines, networking with other organizations, membership in business referral groups, and customer referral networking groups. Childers and Offstein (2007), Ratnasingam (2008), and Suki et al. (2008) found that several organizations are engaged in database marketing, e-marketing, social media, and network marketing to promote or enhance financial performance. According to Porter (2008), business executives' see niche strategies as means of increasing sustainable advantages, market shares, higher sales, better margin, and higher revenue.

Several participants did not believe customers were receiving incentive to ensure repeat purchase. Most participants stated that online managers in their company did not explain how to use risk assessment. In contrast, Lin and Wu (2008), Meroño-Cerdán (2008), and Ratnasingam (2008) argued that success with customer acquisition and retention leads to profitability. In marketing practice-performance relationship, Khalifa and Liu (2007), Coviello et al. (2006), and Chong (2008) discussed customer relationship and the advantages that result from such an activity. Palvia and D'Aubeterre (2007), Gardner (2007), and Suki et al. (2008) argued that online customer retention strategy is imperative for profitability.

Garrity et al. (2007), and Gengatharen and Standing (2005) discovered that customer retention is positively correlated with interaction marketing; on the contrary, customer acquisition is positively correlated with both interaction marketing, and transaction marketing. Management may use interaction form of relational marketing to implement offensive and defensive strategy. Lin and Wu (2008), Coviello et al. (2006), and Beck and Franke (2008), found that customer acquisition and retention is positively associated with sales growth and believed that only sales growth and customer retention is positively correlated with profitability.

A few participants believed that e-commerce organizations had become very popular. The business owners believed that their profitability models were most likely to succeed. Quinton and Mohammed (2009), and Gofman et al. (2009), and Simpson et al. (2006) argued that business owners are enabling as well as extending product giveaways to enhance brand, optimize profit, generate traffic, and attain sustainable advantages.

Summary

The barriers to the operation of an online business, strategies used to mitigate those barriers, and the methods that were used to maximize profit were identified. These results could help entrepreneurs to standardize procedures, maximize revenue, and sustain a competitive advantage.

According to Yanamandram and White (2006), Doherty and Lockett (2007), and Chong (2008), dissatisfied customers switched to other online companies. Several customers were frustrated when online organizations refused to communicate with customers about delayed shipments. Additional reasons for customer dissatisfaction were failure to meet customer expectations, and not being responsible for problems caused by the service provider.

A high level summary of the findings were developed for the three themes that emerged from the current study. Three major themes and findings emerged about the barriers to online business profitability for small businesses. The following findings and themes that address the six research questions were integrated from the data collected with the face-to-face, email, telephone and follow up interviews.

Findings related to research question 1 (What procedures, methods and risk assessments are used to eliminate barriers to online-business sustainable advantages for small business?) The first research question of the study was answered through theme number 1 and associated findings that emerged. The first theme was barriers to the operations of online business. The findings of the study indicated that entrepreneurs had experienced lack of repeat purchase from the online customers. The findings identified that entrepreneurs had no way of registering customers' complaints, eliciting customer opinions or feedback, and using them to encourage repeat purchases. The findings of the study indicated small business owners had not been able to obtain business loans. The study indentified that entrepreneurs were reluctant to be proactive in order to make their company more competitive. The study identified that the main problem was funding, but some entrepreneurs indicated that an occasional face-to-face interaction with prospective customers could add to their online sales. The finding presented in study confirmed lack of communication.

The entrepreneurs remarked that their online organization could not monitor products or their customers' service preferences. The entrepreneurs explained that customer calls and inquiries were not answered promptly. Almost half of the entrepreneurs reported that the lack of face-to-face contact was a problem. The entrepreneurs expressed their views on the difficulty of keeping customers. The entrepreneurs thought that encouraging repeat business was one of their most serious problems.

Business owners held their employees accountable for ensuring the safety, protection and security of customer information on the web site. The finding identified that keeping customer information safe and secure is essential to the success of online business. The finding identified that entrepreneurs could not afford to hire in-house auditors. Nor did the online managers perform risk assessment. The finding of the study was that entrepreneurs have not been able to convince their online customers that their information would be safe.

The finding provided that entrepreneurs did not anticipate that easy to navigate website would raise the company's bottom line. Another finding showed inefficiencies affecting the ease of website navigation. Online managers did not take advantage of the online tools for customers. An important finding that emerged was that managers did not provide website improvement and sustainability. The findings of the study indicated that SMEs websites were not up to date. The finding revealed that organizational websites did not contain the right information.

Findings related to research questions 2 (How are the procedures, methods and risk assessments implemented?), and research questions 3 (How are procedures, methods and risk assessments monitored and verified?) The second and third research questions of the study were answered through theme number 2 and associated findings that emerged. The second theme was strategies used to mitigate those barriers. Business owners had to make sure that their customers had computers and Internet access. The finding was that online SMEs maintained corporate offices to service the needs of the online customers. The finding identified that entrepreneurs hired customer service representatives and integrated open online forums to support online customers. Finding of the current study claimed that online entrepreneurs embedded telephone numbers on the web sites to cope with emergencies or interactions between customers, and online business owners.

Most of the business owners had corporate offices. Business owners stated that the online customers were not invited to visit the office in order to embolden relationship between consumers and organization leaders. Some business owners asserted that they had customer service representatives available by telephone and email, and open online forums for their customers. Small business owners responded that the method implemented was online-sales support but in order to build relationship, the organizational leaders did not invite customers to the offline office due to insurance liability.

The finding of the study identified that investing in state-of-the-art online security software would qualify as a potent strategy for mitigating barriers. Other business owners believed that online managers should mitigate barriers by keeping graphic user (interface) simple and user friendly. Some business owners commented that managers in their company did not hire personnel to monitor website publication, manage website navigation, and reduce sustainability barriers. To mitigate barriers, other business owners recommended that sending sales personnel to neighborhoods to tell people how to buy cheap products on the Internet.

To curb fraud and other anomalies, business owners stated that the policies and procedures of the company were embedded on the web sites discouraging customers to use debit card online; they are free to use Master or Visa credit cards to make their payments. Another business owner stated that the organizational managers requested consumers to call the web site telephone number in order to log complaints on fraud. The finding from entrepreneurs indicated that necessary steps were taken to inform the customers about the protection of their personal dossier, credit cards, and that the website and servers are safeguarded with firewall (or McAfee) software. The entrepreneurs emphasized that small business owners should sell the products the competitors are not proffering to the consumers.

Findings related to research questions 4 and 5 (What are the key problems connected with implementing the procedures, methods and risk assessments to eliminate barriers?), and research question 5 (What primary internal controls (manuals or flow-charts) are used to eradicate barriers?) The fourth and fifth research questions of the study were answered through theme number 2 and associated findings that emerged. The second theme was strategies used to mitigate those barriers. Almost all entrepreneurs concluded that the academic communities should take the burden to write papers highlighting peculiar barriers and proffering technical based solutions to counter barriers. The finding of the study indicated that auditing concepts could help organizational leaders to create and implement internal control manuals (or flow-charts) that may be used to eradicate barriers. Almost all entrepreneurs enumerated that without internal control manuals (or flow-charts), organizations would not be equipped to wage an effective intelligent and result-oriented war on forces of barriers affecting sustainable advantages. Almost all entrepreneurs agreed that the organizational managers were not confident enough to develop standard internal control manuals and flow charts for the company. The leaders did not train employees on the principle of eradicating barriers.

Findings related to research question 6 (What profitability models and/or methods do online small businesses use to generate income?) The sixth research question of the study was answered through theme number 3 and associated findings that emerged. The third theme was methods that were utilized to maximize profit. According to the finding of this study, most entrepreneurs cited the use of economic of scale to maximize profits. Business owners instituted economies of scale to increase total number of student admissions to the school. The business owners believed that the more students admitted to the school, the less the cost per student, and the higher the profitability.

The business owners updated their methods to elicit big retention. The efforts of the business owners were tied to maximization of student enrollment. The business owners engaged massively in advertisement to maximize profit. Additional methods utilized by entrepreneurs to maximize profit were door to door advertisement, online marketing, powerful website, exit splash, and YouTube. The online managers invited their customers to visit the ground location in order to repair their cell phones.

To maximize profit, other business owners were comfortable with the methods regarded as economic of scale, twitter, using exit splash software, and YouTube marketing. The business owners preferred to use search engine optimization, and free advertisement available on the Internet. The analysis of the data from the interview indicated that the business owners had different processes to maximize profit. The business owners were oriented in using sponsorships models, marketing models, and benefit participations models to maximize profit. The findings of the study revealed that business owners maintain modest advertising budget and incorporated the following: print media in entertainment book, Online Links, memorable brand, online marketing, Facebook commerce, and search engine optimization blog. Small-business owners believed blogging provides value for marketing business, however, some small-business owners did not believe online coupon could boost the numbers of shoppers that would navigate, and purchase on their websites.

To expose the brand to consumers, some managers prefer to use blogging marketing, Facebook commerce, online marketing, YouTube and discussion on open forums. The online organizations are embracing YouTube, Facebook commerce, and iPad to develop relationships, transparency, and mutual benefits with consumers. These powerful technological tools could help organizations achieve their anticipated financial goals.

All entrepreneurs reported using methods like Facebook commerce, online marketing, YouTube, open forums, search help desk, product support, Twitter, Flickr from Yahoo, and Atomic blogging to maximize profit. According to the finding of this study, online managers were implementing the company presence in popular search engines to maximize profit. The entrepreneurs informed the study that business owners were using website help to generate leads of potential customers.

According to the finding of this study, most leaders were providing information about the products to targeted customer base. An interesting finding was that online business owners are incorporating Google search engine, Yahoo search engines, networking with other organizations, membership in business referral groups, and customer referral networking groups. In order to maximize profit, the findings of the current study indicated that the managers prefer cost effectiveness, cost control, and proactive marketing approach. However, some managers do it differently; for example, to maximize profit, the online managers prefer to cut expenses, keep cost low, and increase sales by selling quality products.

To maximize profit, the findings showed that business owners advertise with Twitter, banner advertising, MySpace, Blogging, and social networking. Finally, to maximize profit, the findings of the study presented that several online business owners required their workforce to generate higher volume of sales. According to the finding of this study, most online business owner promoted online visibility with Google as their provider. The business owners believed that the profitability models established in their organizations were effective, and most likely to succeed. The findings reflected that the profitability models established can be deemed responsible for lot of sales and revenue. The findings identified that the more money expended to increase awareness to the public, the more enrollments would manifest for the business owners. Most managers prefer advertisements such as television adverts, internet, blogs, YouTube, and popular newspaper advertisement.

Chapter 5

Many owners of SMEs have not conducted risk assessments to secure a competitive advantage (Aziz & Poorsartep, 2009; DotCom Boom, 2005; Gengatharen & Standing, 2005; Loghry & Veach, 2009; Porter, 2008).

Online managers are responsible for ensuring that the SMEs are integrating Internet business solutions to enhance their performance. This qualitative holistic multiple-case study was to ascertain whether procedures, risk assessments and business strategies created sustainable advantages for this category of SMEs. The unit of analysis in this study was the online SMEs market with multiple cases of individual online SMEs. The unit of analysis (20 participants) was selected following purposeful sampling (Zikmund, 2003). The names of the prospective participants were obtained from the United States Chamber of Commerce. This study could help academic communities and prospective entrepreneurs to understand the activities of online SMEs and the importance of eradicating barriers that could prevent sustainable advantages for SMEs in online environment. A qualitative holistic multiple-case study design was appropriate for the current study because significant attributes of the multiple cases were embedded and barriers to online-business profitability for online small businesses in the United States were rigorously explored (Yin, 2009).

The participants were informed about their right to privacy, confidentiality, informed consent and protection of their information. They then signed the informed consent form. To comply with ethical codes, several individual use coding and recording strategies to conceal the names of the participants (Yin, 2009). IRB approval was obtained before data were collected. The confidential data provided by participants were not shared or disclosed.

All participants were assigned code numbers. Compensation was not provided. The participants were also assured of protection from physical harm, emotional harm and coercion. They would incur no reprisals for their refusal to participate and had the right to omit question(s) or withdraw from the study at any time.

A qualitative holistic multiple-case study was conducted to obtain entrepreneurs viewpoints (live experience) on whether procedures, risk assessment and business strategies could create sustainable advantages for SMEs, which had gone online since 2006. The analytical strategies used were pattern matching, rival explanations, and theoretical propositions. In a multiple-case study, Yin (2009) argued that theory is imperative for conducting data collection, processing, and analysis. In a case study design, Yin (2009) posited that the academic communities are known for using pattern matching, explanation building, or logic model to analyze data. In this study, qualitative holistic multiple-case design was organized to achieve the research purpose. Yin stated that any implementation of multiple-case studies should adhere to the concept of replication without adhering to sampling criterion. Yin demonstrated that the academic communities are known to peruse and select each case carefully to elicit validity (2003 and 2009). This qualitative holistic multiple-case study prevents equivocal evidence and preconceived notions from influencing the findings and conclusions (Yin, 2009). In order to elicit rigor, personal biases were prevented from affecting the research (Yin, 2009).

Twenty small business owners were interviewed to identify some of these (barriers, viewpoints, opinion, skills, practices) and the study was informed on how prudent strategies created sustainable advantages for SMEs in online marketplaces. The experiences of 20 SMEs owners who decided to establish an online presence was gathered and reported. In this research, a qualitative software program, Nvivo 8, was used to analyze each participant's interview transcript and the data from the interviews were developed into cogent findings and recommendations (Yin, 2009). The data collected were analyzed and the data were placed under each one of the major three themes that emerged regarding the study. The first theme was barriers to the operation of an online business. The second theme was strategies used to mitigate those barriers. The third theme was methods that were utilized to maximize profit. In this chapter and in chapter 4, many of the findings (themes) were evaluated and compared to previous findings from several scholarly literatures.

Implications

The research questions in this study were answered by online SMEs in the United States. The three themes that emerged were barriers to online business, strategies implemented to mitigate barriers and methods used to maximize profit. The findings may not be applicable to other cities and states in the world. Other research could be undertaken to learn from other participants elsewhere in the world. The research was intended to contribute to and disseminate information about barriers to profitability of online small businesses in the United States. The research consisted of the analysis of problems and logistics in relation to profitability for online small businesses. The qualitative strategies were used to explore barriers to sustainable advantages for SMEs, which had gone online since 2006.

Implications of the findings for research questions were answered in the current study. Implications of the findings for research questions 1 (What procedures, methods and risk assessments are used to eliminate barriers to online-business sustainable advantages for small business?) were as follows. The finding of the study was that online managers did not perform risk assessment to eliminate the barrier of aggressive rivalry of sellers. The business owners did not prevent barriers that may impede the sustainable advantages for SMEs. The findings of the study showed that many organizations could not implement their procedures due to inadequate knowledge of competitors' plans, lack of strategies, and financial shortages. The implication of not conducting risk assessments may result in new barriers, existing barriers enduring, and financial loss. The first research question of the study was answered through theme number 1 and associated findings that emerged. The first theme was barriers to the operations of online business.

Implications of the findings for research questions 2 and 3 (How are the procedures, methods and risk assessments implemented?) and (How are procedures, methods and risk assessments monitored and verified?) were as follows. The finding was that business owners preferred internal controls to eliminate barriers in order to achieve the mission and objectives of organizations. The findings of the study presented that most entrepreneurs were ignorant of the kind of jeopardy imposed upon business by barriers; neither had they any business knowledge of how/when to implement solution to manage risks and barriers. The implications were that adequate procedures and risk assessments were not implemented to create sustainable advantages for online SMEs. Implications of the findings were that lack of funding and knowledge prevented entrepreneurs from integrating procedures and risk assessments. The implication of not monitoring procedures and risk assessments indicated that the leaders are negating the mission and objectives of the SMEs. The implications were that adequate barrier elimination could not be achieved until procedures and risk assessments are monitored and verified. The implications of the findings were inability to effectively monitor procedures, verify risk assessments and manage barriers to sustainable advantages of SMEs. The second and third research questions of the study were answered through theme number 2 and associated findings that emerged. The second theme was strategies used to mitigate those barriers. The second theme pertained to strategies used to mitigate those barriers.

Implications of the findings for research questions 4 and 5 (What are the key problems connected with implementing the procedures and risk assessments to eliminate barriers?) and (What primary internal controls (manuals or flow-charts) are used to eradicate barriers?) were as follows. The finding of the study concerned that without internal control manuals, organizations would not be equipped to wage an effective war on barriers to sustainable advantages. The implications were inability to assess the key problems and implement remedies to eliminate barriers. The finding of the study was that academic communities should take the burden to write papers highlighting peculiar barriers and proffering technical based solutions to counter barriers. Implications of the findings were complexity in identifying key issues to integrating procedures, risk assessments, and eradicate potential barriers. The implication that the entrepreneurs did not standardized internal controls and written guidelines to deter non-compliance, detect barriers and mistakes in a timely manner, and allow corrective actions to be taken swiftly. The implications were inability of managers integrating internal controls. Online managers should implement improved internal controls for tracking and reporting barriers. Managers must enhance internal controls, maximize cash flow and minimize losses. The fourth and fifth research questions of the study were answered through theme number 2 and associated findings that emerged. The second theme was strategies used to mitigate those barriers.

Implications of the findings for research question 6: (What profitability models and/or methods do online small businesses use to generate income?) include the following: The study concludes that successful small business owners integrated economic of scale. Profitability models were not standardized to generate income and enhance market share. The study finds that business owners preferred to use search engine optimization, and free advertising on the Internet. The development of profitability models could provide long-term financial and market growth for online SMEs. An interesting finding was that online business owners promoted online visibility with Google. The lack of awareness of products or services could become an impediment to sustainable advantages for online SMEs. The sixth research question of the study was answered through theme number 3 and associated findings that emerged. The third theme was methods that were utilized to maximize profit.

The research questions determined whether adequate procedures and risk assessments had been implemented. The research questions for the current study were as follows:

Q1: What procedures, methods and risk assessments are used to eliminate barriers to online-business sustainable advantages for small business?

Q2: How are the procedures, methods and risk assessments implemented?

Q3: How are procedures, methods and risk assessments monitored and verified?

Q4: What are the key problems connected with implementing the procedures, methods and risk assessments to eliminate barriers?

Q5: What primary internal controls (manuals or flow-charts) are used to eradicate barriers?

Q6: What profitability models and/or methods do online small businesses use to generate income?

Research Findings from Question 1. What procedures, methods and risk assessments are used to eliminate barriers to online-business sustainable advantages for small businesses? Karakaya and Stahl (2009), Beaver (2007), and Auger (2005) corroborated the present findings by asserting that factors affecting e-commerce resources include lack of technical expertise, interaction, financial funding, inadequate e-commerce infrastructure and high learning curve associated in operating e-commerce. Seven participants identified financial constraints as their most serious problem; two indicated that face-to-face interaction with prospective customers could increase sales. Three participants made the same comment about lack of communication. Ratnasingam (2008), Lin and Wu (2008), and Childers and Offstein (2007) disagreed, contending that innovative small business owners maintain cordial relationships with customers.

Five participants commented about their board membership and banking industry experience. Participants discussed the history of their companies. Participants noted that they had not been able to obtain loans, but were determined to. Karakaya and Stahl (2009), Wresch and Fraser (2006), and Wong (2007) confirmed this, stating that financial industry often refuses to approve loans to small online businesses. In corroboration, Hettche and Walker (2010), Beaver (2007), and Beck and Franke (2008) found that business owners benefit from the relationships with their customers. Small business owners should remember that their customers are their first priority. Murphy et al. (2008), Xu et al. (2007), and Vachon (2011) theorized that when consumers are satisfied, online companies thrive.

Hettche and Walker (2010), Burgess and Tatnall (2007), and Repchuck (2008) posited that online managers could retain customers by providing live telephone conferences, two-way communication, satisfaction, and courtesy. Almost half of the participants mentioned the lack of face-to-face contact as a problem. Hu and Wu (2008), Suki et al. (2008), and Wong (2007) found that the proactive managers are using anti-virus software and auditing process to protect online customers from fraud, risk and data loss. Findings support Hu and Wu (2008), Suki et al. (2008), and Wong (2007).

Research Findings from Questions 2 and 3. How are the procedures, methods, and risk assessments implemented? How are procedures, methods and risk assessments monitored and verified? Offstein and Childers (2008), Beaver (2007), and Ashwin (2006) who found that governments and/or private entities are funding research and development in computer industry to increase cost effectiveness and minimize the cost of personal computers. The business owners confirmed the findings of Karakaya and Stahl (2009), Arcand et al. (2007), and Griffiths and Howard (2008) who theorized that online managers should hire webmasters. A few participants stated that investing in state-of-the-art online security software would protect businesses and their customers. Disagreeing with Karakaya and Stahl (2009), Arcand et al. (2007), and Griffiths and Howard (2008), some participants commented that managers in their company had not hired webmasters. Bharadwaj and Soni (2007), Rau (2007), and Repchuck (2008) asserted that business groups are reassuring customers about threats to online transactions, payment, security and privacy.

Doherty and Lockett (2007), Hettche and Walker (2010), and Khattab et al. (2010) emphasized that online organizations are extending decorum to prospective and current customers by increasing satisfaction, promoting loyalty, and solving problems. Consistent with Doherty and Lockett (2007), Hettche and Walker (2010), and Khattab et al. (2010), most of the participants stated that they have corporate offices. Some participants emphasized that customer service representatives are always available. In contrast to Doherty and Lockett (2007), Hettche and Walker (2010), and Khattab et al.

(2010), participants stated that the online customers were not invited to visit the office by organization leaders.

Dikolli and Sedatole (2007), Khalifa and Liu (2007), and Auger (2005) corroborated the findings by stating that business owners are incorporating customer relations, online help, better products, online chat venues and increased customer outreach to enhance market share and revenue. The participants commented on the availability of customer service, product support and online forums. The findings of the study were inconsistent with those of Dikolli and Sedatole (2007), Khalifa and Liu (2007), and Auger (2005). In concurrence, Lin and Wu (2008), Khattab et al. (2010), and Loukis et al. (2008) explicated that entrepreneurs are known to develop customer policy through sales, training, satisfaction, repurchase, retention, free trials, and discounts. Entrepreneurs should implement, enforce and update the policy. Another participant explained that customer service representatives were not required to tutor computer-illiterate people on Internet navigation.

The managers of SMEs should utilize the strategy of bringing meeting (presentations) to target customers to build more customer base. Beaver (2007), Chong (2008), and Zhuang (2005) agreed that business owners should use the most efficient and economical means of attracting customers while complying with prudent business practices. The participants noted the problem of thin profit margin for online products. Porter (1998 and 2008) asserted that business managers should improve the quality of their products in order to annihilate the cost of conversion to substitutes.

Research Findings from Questions 4 and 5. What are the key problems connected with implementing the procedures, methods and risk assessments to eliminate barriers? What primary internal controls are used to eradicate barriers? Participants cited inadequate knowledge of competitors' plans, lack of strategies and financial constraints. The participants in this study did not corroborate the findings of Dikolli and Sedatole (2007), Beaver (2007), and Auger (2005) who argued that business owners with adequate funding can conduct operations in order to achieve the objectives of the organization. The participants noted that most entrepreneurs were ignorant of the kind of jeopardy imposed upon business by barriers. Managers did not know how and when to implement strategy to eliminate potential barriers. The participants disagreed with Hodges and Kent (2007), Durand (2006), and Beaver (2007) who indicated that successful entrepreneurs believe in preplanning, reducing barriers, attending seminars and viewing videos on marketing-competitive strategies.

Fox (2008), Meroño-Cerdán (2008), and Jansen and Schuster (2011) found that barriers to small businesses had not been the focus of companies because entrepreneurs competing with online SMEs or larger organizations were a new phenomenon. The interview data in this study did not substantiate Fox (2008), Meroño-Cerdán (2008), and Jansen and Schuster (2011) finding. The participants in this study did not support Lin and Wu (2008), Ratnasingam (2008), and Jansen and Schuster (2011) finding that several organizational managers are performing audit engagement on company activities by using internal control strategies. The participants in this study did not corroborate the findings of Ratnasingam (2008), Antlová (2009), and Meroño-Cerdán (2008), who noted that several organizations are profitable because they have consistent operations, policy, controls, skill set, training and strategies.

According to Khattab et al. (2010), Loghry and Veach (2009), and Simpson et al. (2006) risk reduction is an important step on the path to barrier independence. The outcome of a risk assessment must include synopses of potential barriers, financial loss, internal control, monitoring strategies, and suggestion on risk mitigation. The interview responses did not support Khattab et al. (2010), Loghry and Veach (2009), and Simpson et al. (2006). From the participants' perspective, the internal control manuals had not been developed for key areas pertinent. Participants commented that they preferred internal control but that they did not have a written monitoring, and verification policy. Most participants conceded that their organizations did not believe in risk prevention. Yan (2007), Gardner (2007), and Galloway and Mochrie (2005) emphasized that business owners should have internal control policies to reduce potential risks. Data regarding risks should be accumulated in preparation for the formal review; and risk reduction should be implemented.

Research Findings from Question 6. What profitability models and/or methods do online small businesses use to generate income? The efforts of the business owners were tied to maximization of enrollment. Simpson et al. (2006), Palvia and D'Aubeterre (2007), and Repchuck (2008) corroborated the current finding by remarking that several managers in SMEs are in favor of increasing marketing operations and productivity when they need more revenue. When the managers expect their marketing efforts to be rewarded by increased revenue, managers are emboldened to design new products, seek new markets, and increase productivity. Wong (2007), Suki et al. (2008), and Rauyruen et al. (2009) argued that e-commerce advertisement model is an excellent way to optimize and maximize revenue.

These findings contrast with Rauyruen et al. (2009), Khalifa and Liu (2007), and Darbyshire (2008), who stated that business owners are enhancing the quality of their products to promote customer relationship and re-purchase. Ratnasingam (2008), Saastamoinen (2009), and Vachon (2011) demonstrated that managers are adopting customer recognition programs to attain profitability and retain customers. To retain customers, sevcral managers are distributing gratitude certificates, acknowledgement letters, and certificates of appreciation.

To maximize profit, the participants cited online marketing models, market structure, advertisement models, and market share. Another method cited by the business owners were advertisement on search engine, television, and web site. According to several participants, additional methods documented to maximize profit were door to door advertisement, online marketing, powerful website, and YouTube. Some participants stated that the online managers invited their customers to visit the ground location in order to repair their cell phones. Other participants stated that the business owners preferred to use search engine optimization, and free advertisements on the Internet. Wong (2007), Harris and Rae (2009), and Rauyruen et al. (2009) argue that business owners are reaping the benefit of sales volume, cash flow, and cost effectiveness through e-commerce models, and marketing campaigns.

Some participants indicated that their SMEs competed against large businesses with more capital and name recognition. A few participants noted that their websites lacked sufficient traffic. Visser and Weiderman (2011), Suki et al. (2008), and Repchuck (2008) acknowledged that online entrepreneurs should implement the recognizable work or keyword of their products or services on Goggle, Yahoo, MSN, Bing, and other search engines. Small business owners are leveraging social media tools. To converse with the prospective customers and drive traffic to the websites, some entrepreneurs are using websites like halfoffdepot.com, livingsocial.com, saveology.com, plumdistrict.com, shopsocially.com, kactoos.com, groupon.com, stuffbuff.com, and buywithme.com.

The interview data indicated that business owners had different ways of maximizing profit. The participants asserted that business owners did not extend product discounts to persuade consumers to make purchases. Early in the interview sessions, the participants emphasized that they were using sponsorships models, marketing models and other models to maximize profit. Vachon (2011), Rickards (2007), and Wong (2007) explain that entrepreneurs generate revenue by developing business plans and promoting their products or services to current and prospective customers. According to Porter (2008), niche strategies are sources of sustainable advantage, higher net income, higher volumes, transparent publicity, and more profit.

The participants maintained modest advertising budgets that incorporated entertainment books, Online Links, memorable brand, online marketing, Facebook commerce, and search engine optimization blog. Small-business owners believed blogging provides value for marketing business, however, some participants did not believe online coupons could bring them more customers. Wong (2007), Ashwin (2006), Campbell and Wright (2008) maintain that online managers are increasing revenue and market share of their organizations by integrating chat rooms, email, forums, discussion boards, SMS text, video messaging, blogs, and banner advertising.

Many participants stated that the business owners were not advertising with flyers, posters, community-banner, celebrity support, business card and billboards. Some participants stated that managers preferred to use blogs, Facebook commerce, online marketing, YouTube, and discussion forums. Other participants mentioned that the online sales group had the ability to expedite action on online traffic. Ashwin (2006), Jansen and Schuster (2011), MacGregor (2006), and Auger (2005) stated that several managers of e-commerce organizations maximize profit by integrating blogs, banner ads, sponsored links, stickers, badges, spray paint logos, and pavement chalking.

The online organizations are embracing YouTube, Facebook commerce, and iPad to develop relationships, transparency, and mutual benefits with consumers. These powerful technological tools could help organizations achieve their financial goals. All participants reported using methods like Facebook commerce, online marketing, YouTube, open forums, search help desk, product support, blogging, Twitter, Flickr from Yahoo, and Atomic blogging to maximize profit. During the interview, the participants informed the study that business owners were using website help to generate leads.

Some participants stated that online entrepreneurs were providing information about the products to targeted customer base. The participants cited that online sales group had the ability to expedite action on online traffic. McDougall (2006), Campbell and Wright (2008), and Jansen and Schuster (2011) substantiated the present findings by asserting that talented online managers promoted products or services through web- based advertisement models, affiliate marketing, webinars, word press blogs, and social media sites.

One conclusion drawn during this fieldwork was that small business owners had their own methods to maximize profit. For example, Participants 2, 4, and 7 relied on cost effectiveness, cost control, and proactive marketing. However, other participants revealed that some managers preferred to cut expenses, kept costs low, and increased sales by selling quality products. Malaga (2007), MacGregor (2006), and Dembla et al. (2007) remarked that online small business owners should focus on strategic alliances to realize cost effectiveness, lower transaction costs, generate sales, growth, and elicit more revenue. Campbell and Wright (2008), Jansen and

Schuster (2011), and Quinton and Mohammed (2009) in corroboration asserted that entrepreneurs are engaging in online bilateral interactions to obtain customers' feedback.

The participants interviewed were of the opinion that the business owners instituted effective profitability models. A few participants believed that e-commerce organizations had become very popular in their community. The business owners believed that the profitability models established in their organizations were effective, and most likely to succeed. Jansen and Schuster (2011), Campbell and Wright (2008), and Auger (2005) opined that managers were enabling varieties of online affiliate marketing, online discussions of products, and advertisement model to maximize profit. According to Porter (2008), the managers were implementing the following profitability methods to attain sustainable advantages: product differentiation, lowest-cost business operations, online networking, and branding.

Recommendations

Online small business owners are at risk of financial hemorrhage; as a result, the following recommendations are presented. Small business owners should participate in profit maximization seminars and aim to improve profitability by networking or obtaining customer referral from other SMEs. Online entrepreneurs should promote their products and services by implementing social shopping, and using social media. The entrepreneurs should conduct annual risk assessments and risk management. Online small business owners have internal controls to reduce barriers, maximize revenue, and control expenditures. The entrepreneurs should use Microsoft Office Access to document the internal control database for preventing barriers.

The recommendation provides that the entrepreneurs of online SMEs should develop indexing of methods to eliminate potential barriers (or current barricrs) to online-business profitability for small businesses. The entrepreneurs should join an online barrier reducing association that discusses strategies to mitigate barriers for online small businesses in United States. The association of online SMEs should create directory of online businesses (home page or universal resource locator), similar to telephone yellow pages booklet and distribute the booklet to houses in United States.

The entrepreneurs of online SMEs should conduct periodic risk assessments, develop audit plan and eliminate barriers. These managers should engage certified internal auditors to perform e-commerce audit engagement to determine the adequacy of the strategies implemented to eliminate barriers. In order to accomplish this and be in compliance with professional auditing standards, the findings and recommendations must be issued via formal audit report projects performed by the internal auditors. Using internal auditors provides several SMEs owners clear direction and foundation for remediation and future communication. The online entrepreneurs should indicate how the issues identified were resolved.

The online SMEs should encourage all the stakeholders/employees to carry and distribute the companies' business cards. Online small business owners should undergo continuous profit maximizing training programs. These entrepreneurs should purchase online profit making videos and watch videos illustrating various methods to maximize profits. The online SMEs should conduct monthly inexpensive birthday celebrations for their stakeholders, employees and online customers; an excellent strategy is to invite those online customers with birthdays coinciding within those months to attend at the local office for joint birthday celebrations. Online entrepreneurs should seize the opportunity of the monthly birthday celebrations to encourage questions, obtain feedback from the customers, extend gifts, enhance customers care, and build relationship.

Conclusions

The themes of this study are the barriers to online business, strategies implemented to mitigate barriers, and methods used to maximize profit. This chapter summarized the problem statement, purpose, methodology, limitations, and significance of the study. The findings will enable entrepreneurs to create profitable online small businesses. Further, this chapter discussed the implications of this study, three research findings that addressed the six research questions, the contributions of the study to the scholarly literature, and several recommendations for owners of small online businesses in the United States.

The findings of the study indicated that an occasional face-to-face interaction with prospective customers could augment sales for an online company. The findings presented in study confirmed lack of communication, customers voice messages, calls, emails, and letters were not answered on a timely basis indicative of the barriers confronting the online company. These entrepreneurs were unable to retain customers and perform risk assessment. The managers did not realize that user-friendly websites would raise the bottom line of the company. An important finding was that entrepreneurs did not provide website improvement, and keeping website up to date on current products.

ABOUT THE AUTHOR

Dr. Ebenezer Robinson was awarded his Ph.D. in Business Administration and Electronic Commerce from Northcentral University, Prescott Valley, Arizona. Prior to that, he had earned a Master of Business Administration (MBA) with concentration in Management and Business from American Inter-Continental University, Houston, Texas. His undergraduate work was at California State University Dominguez Hills, Carson, CA, where he earned a Bachelor of Science degree in Business Administration with specialization in Accounting. Dr. Robinson is committed to life-long learning.

The focal point for Dr. Robinson's work is in building people, students, adults, teams, stakeholders and organizations as "learning systems" designed for sustainable development. Dr. Ebenezer A. Robinson is primarily a business, management, e-commerce, auditing, and accounting policy analyst with strong albeit secondary interest in academia. This explains his involvement as a professor of business and management at the University in USA. Dr. Robinson is passionate about helping students to learn and pursue their bachelor, masters or doctoral degrees.

Dr. Robinson reinvented himself by acquiring knowledge and research experience in a Ph.D. program in Business Administration and Electronic Commerce. Robinson is a research scientist who possesses teaching, writing, researching, managing, consulting, and entrepreneuring experience. He had published over 8 publications and presented 5 papers at several professional and scholarly meetings. In addition to his degrees, he is also a Certified Master Project Manager (MPM), and a Certified Master Financial Manager (MFM). Robinson has over 30 years of Corporate America experience in upper-level management, executive director, business management, and accounting management.

References

Adekunle, P., & Tella, A. (2008). Nigeria SMEs participation in electronic economy: Problems and the way forward. *Journal of Internet Banking and Commerce, 13*(3), 1-13. doi: 1657609701

Allen, R. G., J. (2006). *Multiple stream of Internet income: How ordinary people make extraordinary money online.* New York, NY: Wiley.

Antlová, K. (2009). Motivation and barriers of ICT adoption in small and medium-sized enterprises. *E+M Ekonomie a Management,*(2), 140-155. doi:1743680191

Apigian, C. H., Ragu-Nathan, B. S., Ragu-Nathan, T. S., & Kunnathur, A. (2005). Internet technology: The strategic imperative. *Journal of Electronic Commerce Research,* 6(2), 123-141. doi: 1065501351

Arcand, M., Nantel, J., Dufour, M. A., & Vincent, A. (2007). The impact of reading a Website's privacy statement on perceived control over privacy and perceived trust. *Online Information*

Review, 31(5), 661. doi: 1363699201

Archer, N. Wang, S., & Kang, C. (2008). Barriers to the adoption of online supply chain solutions in small and medium enterprises. *Supply Chain Management, 13*(1), 73-82. doi: 1440894691

Arest, A., Markellou, P., Mousourouli, I., Sirmakessis, S., & Tsakalidis, A. (2007). A movie e-shop recommendation model based on web usage and ontological data. *Journal of Electronic Commerce in Organizations, 5*(3), 17-34. doi: 1522689711

Ashwin, A. (2006). Guerrilla marketing. *Teaching Busi ness & Economics, 10*(3), 5-7. doi: 1174529301

Ashworth, C. J., Schmidt, R. A., Pioch, E. A., & Hallsworth, A. (2006). Web-weaving: An approach to sustainable e-retail and online advantage in lingerie fashion marketing. *International Journal of Retail & Distribution Management, 34*, 497-511. doi: 1073444591

Audretsch, D. B., & Lehmann, E. (2006). Entrepreneurial access and absorption of knowledge spillovers: Strategic board and managerial composition for competitive advantage. *Journal of Small Business Management, 44*(2), 155-166. doi: 1015558011

Auger, P. (2005). The impact of interactivity and design sophistication on the performance of commercial web sites for small businesses. *Journal of Small Business Management, 43*(2), 119-137. doi: 815638531

Aziz, K., & Poorsartep, M. (2009). Developing the e-Business sector: An exploratory study of the multimedia super corridor (MSC) e-Business Flagship. *The Business Review, Cambridge, 13*(1), 184-192. doi: 1778504831

Bansal, H. S., McDougall, G. H. G., Dikolli, S. S., & Sedatole, K. L. (2004). Relating e-satisfaction to behavioral outcomes: an empirical study. The *Journal of Services Marketing, 18*, 290-302. doi: 702886521

Beaver, G. (2007). The strategy payoff for smaller enter prises. *The Journal of Business Strategy, 28*(1), 11-17. doi: 1181914561

Beck, R., & Franke, J. (2008). Designing reputation and trust management systems. *Journal of Electronic Commerce in Organizations, 6*(4), 8-29. doi: 1559946861

Bharadwaj, P., & Soni, R. (2007). E-commerce usage and perception of e-commerce issues among small firms: Results and implications from an empirical study. *Journal of Small Business Management, 45*, 501-521. doi: 1378966641

Bowen, G. A. (2005). Preparing a qualitative research-based dissertation: Lessons learned. *The Qualitative Report, 10*(2), 208-222. Retrieved from http://www.nova.edu/ssss/QR/QR10-2/bowen.pdf.

Burgess, S., & Tatnall, A. (2007). A business-revenue model for horizontal portals. *Business Process Management Journal, 13*, 662-676. doi: 1337646811

Bradlow, E.T., & Schmittlein, D. C., (2000). The little en gines that could: Modeling the performance of world wide web search engines. *Marketing Science* 19.1, 43-62

Cassar, G., & Gibson, B. (2007). Forecast rationality in small firms. *Journal of Small Business Management, 45,* 283-302. doi:1294062391

Campbell, D. E., & Wright, R. T., (2008). Shut-up I do not care: understanding the role of relevance and interactivity on customer attitudes toward repetitive online advertising. *Journal of Electronic Commerce Research: Online Advertising and Sponsored Search, 9*(1), 62-76. doi: 1439585021

Cattani, K., Perdikaki, O., & Marucheck, A. (2007). The perishability of online grocers. *Decision Sciences, 38,* 329-355. doi: 1286573381

Childers Jr, J. S., & Offstein, E. (2007) Building entrepreneurial e-commerce competitive advantage: A blending of theory and practice. Advances in Competitiveness Research, *15*(1/2), 41-53. doi: 1294069411

Chitura, T., Mupemhi, S., Dube, T., & Bolongkikit, J. (2008). Barriers to electronic commerce adoption in small and medium enterprises: A critical literature review. Review of medium being reviewed title of work reviewed in italics. *Journal of Internet Banking and Commerce,* (2), 1-13. doi:1568124231

Choi, D. H., Kim, C. M., Kim, S., & Kim, S. H. (2006). Customer loyalty and disloyalty in internet retail stores: Its antecedents and its effect on customer price sensitivity. *International Journal of Management, 23,* 925-941,944. doi:1197221341

Chong, S. (2008). Success in electronic commerce implementation: A cross-country study of small and medium-sized enterprises. *Journal of Enterprise Information Management, 21,* 468-492. doi: 1564133921

Chong, S., & Pervan, G. (2007). Factors influencing the extent of deployment of electronic commerce for small-and medium-sized enterprises. *Journal of Electronic Commerce in Organizations, 5*(1), 1-29. doi:1157661671

Comm, J. (2006). *The Adsense Code: What Google never told you about making money with Adsense.* Garden City, NY: Morgan James.

Community Investment Program. (2009). *Definitions of eligible areas.* Retrieved from http://www.fhlbi.com/housing/cipdefea.asp.

Constantinides, E. (2004). Strategies for surviving the Internet meltdown: The case of two Internet incumbents. *Management Decision, 42*(1/2), 89-107. doi: 625827351

Coviello, N., Winklhofer, H. & Hamilton, K. (2006). Marketing practices and performance of small service firms: An examination in the tourism accommodation sector. *Journal of Service Research: JSR, 9*(1), 38-58. doi: 1083568041

Creswell, J. W. (2003). *Research design: Qualitative, quantitative, and mixed.* Thousand Oaks, CA:

Sage.

Creswell, J. W. (2007). *Qualitative inquiry and research design: Choosing among   the five approaches* (2nd ed.). Thousand Oaks, CA: Sage.

Creswell, J. W. (2009). *Research design: Qualitative, quantitative, and mixed* (3rd ed.). Thousand Oaks, CA: Sage.

Darbyshire, P. (2008). Adding value to SMEs in the courier industry by adopting a web-based service delivery model. *Journal of Electronic Commerce in Organizations, 6*(4), 47-76. doi: 1559946871

Dembla, P. Palvia, P., & Krishnan, B. (2007). Understanding the adoption of web-enabled transaction processing by small businesses. *Journal of Electronic Commerce Research, 8*(1), 1-17. doi: 1230897421

Dikolli, S. S. & Sedatole, K. L. (2007). Improvements in the information content of nonfinancial forward-looking performance measures: A taxonomy and empirical application. *Journal of Management Accounting Research, 19*, 71-104. doi:1410539761

Doherty, N. F., & Lockett, N. J. (2007). Closing the gap between the expectations of relationship marketing and the reality of E-CRM. *International Journal of E-Business Research, 3*(2), I, II, III, IV, V, VI. doi: 1310337761

DotCom boom and bust. (2005). *Strategic direction, 21*(2), 30-31. doi: 794096871

Durand, P. A. (2006). Business finance: Estimating start-

up costs for an online business.
Retrieved from
http://www.associatedcontent.com/article/
17858/business_finance_estimating_startup.html
?cat=3

Dawson, A., & Hamilton, V, (2006). Optimizing metadata
to make high-value content
more accessible to Google users. *Journal of
Documentation,* 62.3 307-327

E-commerce slows again. (2008). E-commerce law &
strategy. Retrieved from
http://find.galegroup.com.proxyl.NO.edu/itx/star
t.do?

Eikebrokk, T., & Olsen, D. (2009). Training, competence,
and business performance: evidence from E-
business in European small and medium-sized
enterprises. *International Journal of E-Business
Research,* 5(1), 92-116.   doi: 1588794831

Encyclopedia Britannica. (2009). Online business.
Retrieved from http://www.search
.eb.com/eb/article-9001469

Eysenck, M. (2004). *Research methods design of
investigations. Psychology: An international
perspective.* New York, NY: Psychology Press.

Fox, S. (2008). Internet riches: *The simple money-
making secrets of online millionaires.* New York,
NY: American Management Association.

Galloway, L. (2007). Can broadband access rescue the
rural economy? *Journal of Small*

Business and Enterprise Development, 14, 641-653. doi: 1381002571

Galloway, L., & Mochrie, R. (2005). The use of ICT in ru ral firms: A policy-orientated literature re view. Info: *The Journal of Policy, Regulation and Strategy for Telecommunications, Information and Media, 7*(3), 33-46. doi: 850972961

Gardner, R. (2007). *Make a fortune promoting other people's stuff online: How affiliate marketing can make you rich* (1st ed.). New York, NY: McGraw-Hill.

Garrity, E., O'Donnell, J., Kim, Y., & Sanders, G. (2007). An extrinsic and intrinsic motivation-based model for measuring consumer shopping oriented web site success. *Journal of Electronic Commerce in Organizations, 5*(4), 18-38. doi: 1522689851

Gengatharen, D. E., & Standing, C. (2005). A framework to assess the factors affecting success or failure of the implementation of government-supported regional e-marketplaces for SMEs. *European Journal of Information Systems, 14,* 417-433. doi: 987724721

Golafshani, N. (2003). Understanding reliability and validity in qualitative research. *The Qualitative Report, 8*(4), 597-606. Retrieved from http://www.nova.edu/ssss/QR/QR8-4/golafshani.pdf.

Griffiths, G. H., & Howard, A. (2008). Balancing clicks and bricks - strategies for multichannel retailers. *Journal of Global Business*

Issues, 2(1), 69-75. doi: 1454513921

Guerrero, M. M., Egea, J. M. O., & González, M.V. R. (2007). Characterization of online shoppers with navigation problems. *Direct Marketing, 1*(2), 102-113. doi: 1519866571

Gofman, A, Moskowitz H. R & Mets, T. (2009) Integrat ing science into web design: consumer-driven web site optimization. *The Journal of Consumer Marketing*, 26.4 286-298.

Gluhovsky, I. (2009). Customer behavior model for quality-of-service environments with many service levels. *Journal of Electronic Commerce Research*, 10(1), 29-41. doi: 1667036961

Harris, L., & Rae, A. (2009). The revenge of the gifted amateur... be afraid, be very afraid... *Journal of Small Business and Enterprise Development*, 16(14), 964-709 doi:1927011541

Hettche, M., & Walker, P. (2010). B-Harmony: Building small business and small non- profits partnerships that thrive (*A Framework for Collaborative Competition*). Competition forum, 8(1), 86-93. doi: 2174752241

Hodges, H. E., & Kent, T. W. (2007). Impact of planning and control sophistication in small business. *Journal of Small Business Strategy, 17*(2), 75-87. doi: 1180334021

Hong, I. B. (2007). A survey of Web site success metrics used by Internet-dependent organizations in Korea. *Internet Research, 17*, 272-290. doi: 1281932681

Hu, X., & Wu, Y. (2008). Can web seals work wonders for small e-vendors in the online trading environment? A theoretical approach. *International Journal of E-Business Research, 4*(3), 20-39. doi: 1475965381

Investopedia. (2009). *Profit*. Retrieved May 30, 2009, from http://www.investopedia.com/terms/p/profit.asp.

Johnston, D. A., Wade, M., & McClean, R. (2007). Does e-business matter to SMEs? A comparison of the financial impacts of internet business solutions on European and North American SMEs. *Journal of Small Business Management, 45*(3), 354-361. doi: 1294062421

Jansen, B. J., & Schuster, S. (2011). Bidding on the buy ing funnel for sponsored search and keyword advertising. *Journal of Electronic Commerce Research* 12. 1, 1-18.

Karakaya, F., & Stahl, M. (2009). After market entry bar riers in e-commerce markets. *Journal of Electron ic Commerce Research, 10*(3), 130-143. doi: 1864032831

Khalifa, M. & Liu, V. (2007). Online consumer retention: contingent effects of online shopping habit and online shopping experience. *European Journal of Information Systems*: Including a Special Section on Healthcare Information, 16(6), 780-792. doi: 1399647451.

Kartiwi, M., & MacGregor, R. (2007). Electronic com

merce adoption barriers in small to medium-sized enterprises (SMEs) in developed and developing countries: A cross-country comparison. *Journal of Electronic Commerce in Organizations, 5*(3), 35-51. doi: 1522689731

Kent, P. & Finlayson, J. M. (2006). *How to make money online with eBay, Yahoo and Google* (1st ed.). Emeryville, CA: McGraw-Hill.

Khattab, A. A., Aldehayat, J., & Stein, W. (2010). Inform ing country risk assessment in international business. *International Journal of Business and Management, 5*(7), 54. doi:821543352.

Khalifa, M. & Liu, V. (2007). Online consumer retention: contingent effects of online shopping habit and online shopping experience. *European Journal of Information Systems*: Including a Special Section on Healthcare Information, 16(6), 780-792. doi: 1399647451

Laudon, K. C., & Traver, C. G. (2006). *E-commerce, business, technology and society* (3rd ed.). Upper Saddle River, NJ: Prentice Hall.

Leedy, P. D., & Ormrod, J. E. (2005). *Practical research: Planning and design* (8th ed.). Upper Saddle River, NJ: Pearson.

Lightfoot, W. (2003). Multi-channel mistake: The demise of a successful retailer. International *Journal of Retail & Distribution Management, 31*, 220-229. doi: 345186921

Loukis, E., Sapounas, I., & Aivalis, K. (2008). The effect of generalized competition and strategy on the business value of information and communication technologies. *Journal of Enterprise Information Management*, 21(1), 24-38. doi: 1440904631

Lin, C. P., & Ding, C. G. (2006). Evaluating group differences in gender during the formation of relationship quality and loyalty in ISP service. *Journal of Organizational and End User Computing, 18*(2), 38-62. doi: 1007709521

Lin, Y., & Wu, H. Y. (2008). Information privacy concerns, government involvement, and corporate policies in the customer relationship management context. *Journal of Global Business and Technology, 4*(1), 79-91. doi: 1524926891

Loghry, J. D., & Veach, C. B. (2009). Enterprise risk as sessments: Holistic approach provides companywide perspective. *Professional Safety, 54*(2), 31. doi:200325280

MacGregor, R. C. (2006). The role of strategic alliances in the ongoing use of electronic commerce technology in regional small business. *Journal of Electronic Commerce in Organizations, 2*(1), 1-14. Retrieved doi: 730820071

MacGregor, R. C., & Vrazalic L. (2006). E-commerce adoption barriers in small businesses and the differential effects of gender. *Journal of Electronic Commerce in Organizations, 4*(2), 1-24. doi: 1011183921

Matlay, H. (2004). E-entrepreneurship and small e-business development: towards a comparative research agenda. *Journal of Small Business and Enterprise Development, 11*(3), 408-414. doi: 715297481

Malaga, R. (2007, July/September). The value of search engine optimization: An action research project at a new e-commerce site. *Journal of Electronic Commerce in Organizations*5.3 (July-Sep 2007): 68-82.

McDougall, J. S. (2006). *Start your own blogging business by entrepreneur press, entrepreneur press staff*. New York, NY: McGraw-Hill.

Meroño-Cerdán, A. (2008). Groupware uses and influence on performance in SMEs. The *Journal of Computer Information Systems, 48*(4), 87-96. doi: 1550208091

Mok, J. H. & Vitale, J. (2005). *The e-code: 32 Internet superstars reveal 43 ways to make money online almost instantly using only email*. Hoboken, NJ: John Wiley.

Murphy, H., Catherine, K., & Christian, D. (2008). Do small and medium-sized hotels exploit search engines marketing? *International Journal of Contemporary Hospitality Management* 20. 90-97

O'Dwyer, M., & Ledwith, A. (2009). Determinants of new product performance in small firms. *International Journal of Entrepreneurial Behaviour & Research, 15*(2), 124-136. doi: 1882529121

Offstein, E., & Childers, J. (2008). Small business e-commerce adoption through a qualitative lens: Theory and observations. *Journal of Small Business Strategy, 19*(1), 32-50. doi: 1675597291

Palvia, P., & D'Aubeterre, F. (2007). Examination of in fomediary roles in B2C e-commerce. *Journal of Electronic Commerce Research, 8*, 207-220. doi: 1388674851

Pandya, A. M., & Dholakia, N. (2005). B2C failures: To ward an innovation theory framework. *Journal of Electronic Commerce in Organizations, 3*(2), 68-81. doi: 800939991

Patton, M.Q (2002). *Qualitative research & evaluative methods* (3rd ed.). Thousand Oaks, CA: Sage

Porter, M. (1980a, September-October). How competition forces shape strategy. *Harvard Business Review*, pp.137-145.

Porter, M. (1998) *Competitive strategy: Techniques for analyzing industries and competitors*. New York, NY: Free Press.

Porter, M. E. (2008). The five competitive forces that shape strategy. Harvard Business Review: *Special HBS Centennial Issue, 86*(1), 78-93. doi: 1406854351

Quader, S., & Quader, R. (2008).The utilization of e-commerce by traditional supermarkets in the UK through strategic alliances with Internet based companies. *Journal of Services Research, 8*(1), 177-211. doi: 1548477091

Quinton, S., & Mohammed, A. K. (2009). Generating web
     site traffic: a new model for
     SMEs: An international journal. *Journal of
     Research in Interactive Marketing,* 3.2 109-123.

Raja, J., & Velmurgan, M. S. (2008). E-payments:
     Problems and Prospects. *Journal of Internet
     Banking and Commerce, 13*(1), 1-17.
     doi: 1502828801

Rajagopalan, B., & Deshmukh, A. (2005). Issues and
     advances in B2C research. *Journal of Electronic
     Commerce Research, 6*(2), 75-78. doi: 1065501311

Rau, K. H (2007). Transformation from Internet portal to
     the world's largest Internet communications
     enterprise. *Internet Research, 17*(4), 435-456.
     doi: 1323743861.

Rauyruen, P., Miller, K. E., & Groth, M. (2009). B2B ser
     vices: linking service loyalty
     and brand equity. *The Journal of Services
     Marketing,* 23(3), 175-186. doi: 1879727251

Ranganathan, C., Shetty, A., & Muthukumaran,
     G. (2004). E-business transformation at the
     crossroads: Sears' dilemma. *Journal of
     Information Technology, 19*(2), 117-129.
     doi: 706618371

Ratnasingam, P. (2008). The impact of e-commerce
     customer relationship management in business-
     to-consumer e-commerce. *Journal of Electronic
     Commerce in Organizations, 6*(4), 30-46.
     doi: 1559946851

Raymond, L., & Bergeron, F. (2008). Enabling the business strategy of SMEs through e-business capabilities: A strategic alignment perspective. Industrial Management + Data Systems, *108*(5), 577-595. doi: 1497860951

Repchuck, T. (2008). *31 days to millionaire marketing miracles* (2nd ed.). Burbank CA: Innersurf.

Richards, R.V., & Brown, B. C. (2006). *Online marketing success stories: Insider secrets from the experts who are making millions on the Internet today.* Ocala, FL: Atlantic.

Rickards, R. C. (2007). BSC and benchmark development for an e-commerce SME. Benchmarking, *14*(2), 222-250. doi: 1247983671

Robicheaux, S., & Herrington, C. (2007). Google's Dutch auction initial public offering. *Journal of the International Academy for Case Studies*, 7-19. doi: 1301954171

Rovenpor, J. (2003). Explaining the e-commerce shakeout: Why did so many Internet-based businesses fail? *E - Service Journal, 3*(1), 53-76. doi: 653409511

Saastamoinen, J. (2009). Returns on reputation in retail e-commerce. *Journal of Electronic Commerce Research, 10*(4), 196-219. doi: 1923991451

Schaupp, L. C., & Bélanger, F. (2005). A conjoint analysis of online consumer satisfaction1. *Journal of Elec tronic Commerce Research, 6*(2), 95-111.

doi: 1065501331

Schmelz, D. R. D., & Kennedy, K. N. (2004). Buyer-seller relationships and information sources in an e-commerce world. The *Journal of Business & Industrial Marketing, 19*(3), 188-196. doi: 641708751

Shank, G. D. (2006). *Qualitative research: A personal skills approach* (2nd ed.). Upper Saddle River, NJ: Pearson Merrill Prentice Hall.

Shook, S. R., Vlosky, R. P. & Kallioranta, S. M. (2004). Why did forest industry dot.coms fail? *Forest Products Journal, 54*(10), 35-40. doi: 724484931

Shergill, G. S., & Chen, Z. (2005). Web-based shopping: Consumers' attitudes towards online shopping in New Zealand. *Journal of Electronic Commerce Research, 6*(2), 79-89, 91-94. Retrieved ProQuest database. doi: 1065501321

Silver, D. (2007). *Smart start-ups: How entrepreneurs and corporations can profit by starting online communities.* Hoboken, NJ: John Wiley.

Simpson, M., & Docherty, A. J. (2004). E-commerce adoption support and advice for UK SMEs. *Journal of Small Business and Enterprise Development, 11*, 315-328. doi: 715283251

Simpson, M., Padmore, J., Taylor, N., & Frecknall-Hughes, J. (2006). Marketing in small and medium sized enterprises. *International Journal of Entrepreneurial Behaviour & Research, 12*, 361-364. doi: 1146614641

Smith, A. D. (2005). Reverse logistics programs: gauging their effects on CRM and online behavior. VINE, *35*(3), 166-181. doi: 940309591

Smolander, K., & Rossi, M. (2008). Conflicts, compromises, and political decisions: Methodological challenges of enterprise-wide e-business architecture creation. *Journal of Database Management, 19*(1), 19-40. doi: 1521822071

Suki, N. M., Ramayah, T., & Suki, N. M. (2008). Internet shopping acceptance: Examining the influence of intrinsic versus extrinsic motivations. Direct Marketing, *2*(2), 97-110. doi: 1519866691

Stambaugh, J. E., Yu, A., & Dubinsky, A., J. (2011, February). Before the Attack: A Typology of strategies for competitive aggressiveness. *Journal of Management Policy and Practice* 12(1) 49-63.

Taylor, M., & Murphy, A. (2004). SMEs and e-business. *Journal of Small Business and Enterprise Development, 11*, 280-289. doi: 715282641

Trochim, W., & Donnelly, J. (2007). *The research methods knowledge base*. Mason,OH: Thomson Learning.

Vachon, F. (Oct 2011). Can online decision aids support non-cognitive web shopping approaches? 16-27.

Visser, E. B., & Weiderman, M. (2011). An empirical study on website usability elements and how they affect search engine optimization. *South Africa Journal of Information Management* 13.1 (2011):

C1-C9. Rd

Williams, B. (2007). *How to open and operate a financially successful Web-based business*. Ocala, FL: Atlantic.

Winch G., & Joyce, P (2006). Exploring the dynamics of building, and losing, consumer trust in B2C eBusiness. *International Journal of Retail & Distribution Management: E-commerce, 34*, 541-555. doi: 1073444621

Wong, H. Y. (2007). Using robustness analysis to structure online marketing and communication problems. The *Journal of the Operational Research Society, 58*, 633-644. doi: 1255209231

Wresch, W., & Fraser, S. (2006). Managerial strategies used to overcome technological hurdles: A review of e-commerce efforts used by innovative Caribbe an managers. *Journal of Global Information Management, 14*(3), 1-7,9-16. doi: 1060168541

Xu, M., Rohatgi, R., & Duan, Y. (2007). E-business adoption in SMEs: Some preliminary findings from electronic components industry. *International Journal of E-Business Research, 3*(1), 74-79, 81-90. doi: 1310337881

Yan, R. (2007). Market information strategies for online retailers: Special Issue: Informs revenue management and pricing, *Journal of Revenue and Pricing Management, 6*, 200-211. doi: 1372364721

Yan, R., & Bhatnagar, A. (2008). Product choice strategy for online retailers. International *Journal of E-Business Research, 4*(1), 22-39. doi: 1375024561

144

Yanamandram, V., & White, L. (2006). Switching barriers in business-to-business services: a qualitative study. *International Journal of Service Industry Management, 17*(2), 158-192. doi: 1039659461

Yin, K. R. (2009). *Case study research: Design and methods* (4th ed.). Thousand Oaks, CA: Sage.

Zhuang, Y. (2005). Does electronic business create value for firms? An organizational innovation perspec tive. *Journal of Electronic Commerce Re search,* 6(2), 146-151,153-156. doi: 1065501361

Zikmund, W. (2003). *Business research methods.* Mason, OH: Thomson Learning.

www.ingramcontent.com/pod-product-compliance
Lightning Source LLC
Chambersburg PA
CBHW051709170526
45167CB00002B/603